MARTIN TAYLOR
SINGLE NOTE SOLOING
FOR JAZZ GUITAR

The Complete Guide to Melodic Jazz Guitar Improvisation

MARTIN **TAYLOR**

FUNDAMENTAL**CHANGES**

Martin Taylor Single Note Soloing For Jazz Guitar

The Complete Guide to Melodic Jazz Guitar Improvisation

ISBN: 978-1-78933-088-5

Published by **www.fundamental-changes.com**

Copyright © 2019 Martin Taylor & Joseph Alexander

Edited by Tim Pettingale

The moral right of this author has been asserted.

www.fundamental-changes.com

Twitter: @guitar_joseph

Over 10,000 fans on Facebook: **FundamentalChangesInGuitar**

Instagram: **FundamentalChanges**

For over 350 Free Guitar Lessons with Videos Check Out

www.fundamental-changes.com

Cover Image Copyright: Adam Bulley, used with permission.

Contents

About the Authors

Dr Martin Taylor MBE is a virtuoso guitarist, composer, educator and musical innovator.

Acoustic Guitar magazine has called him, "THE acoustic guitarist of his generation." Chet Atkins said that Martin is, "One of the greatest and most impressive guitarists in the world," and Pat Metheny commented that, "Martin Taylor is one of the most awesome solo guitar players in the history of the instrument."

Widely considered to be the world's foremost exponent of solo jazz and fingerstyle guitar playing, Martin possesses an inimitable style that has earned him global acclaim from fellow musicians, fans and critics alike. He dazzles audiences with a signature style which artfully combines his virtuosity, emotion and humour with a strong, engaging stage presence.

Martin has enjoyed a remarkable musical career spanning five decades, with more than 100 recordings to his credit. Completely self-taught, beginning at the early age of 4, he has pioneered a unique way of approaching solo jazz guitar that he now breaks down into seven distinct stages in order to teach others.

Joseph Alexander is one of the most prolific writers of modern guitar tuition methods.

He has sold over 500,000 books that have educated and inspired a generation of upcoming musicians. His uncomplicated tuition style is based around breaking down the barriers between theory and performance, and making music accessible to all.

Educated at London's Guitar Institute and Leeds College of Music, where he earned a degree in Jazz Studies, Joseph has taught thousands of students and written over 40 books on playing the guitar.

He is the managing director of *Fundamental Changes Ltd.*, a publishing company whose sole purpose is to create the highest quality music tuition books and pay excellent royalties to writers and musicians.

Fundamental Changes has published over 120 music tuition books and is currently accepting submissions from prospective authors and teachers of all instruments. Get in touch via **webcontact@fundamental-changes.com** if you'd like to work with us on a project.

Introduction

Whenever I start to talk about jazz improvisation, I often see my guitar students get nervous, and it's no wonder when you consider how jazz soloing tends to be taught these days. There are so many "rules" and "proper" ways to do things that people can feel intimidated – faced with an incredible mass of theory that they're somehow supposed to play musically.

Many of you will have been taught that the route into authentic jazz soloing is through learning theory and somehow instantly knowing the correct scales and arpeggio substitutions you should play on a Gb7#9b13 chord. (Then, of course, turning all that knowledge into a hip-sounding musical idea for two beats at 180bpm!) I don't know about you, but I break into a cold sweat and feel nauseous just thinking about music that way.

What I want to do in this book is teach you a more musical way to improvise, using a method that grows organically out of the melody of any song and is tightly woven into the tune's structure.

We've all been gigs where it seems as though the melody of a tune is a mere formality. It's gotten out of the way as quickly as possible, so that the cerebral jazz solos can begin – and we've lost all sense of the tune in seconds. I want to show you another way. A way that uses the melody of the tune as the *source* of the solo; a way that doesn't require mind-boggling quantum physics to understand; and, above all, a traditional way of soloing that's been handed down through generations of jazz legends and that I feel privileged to pass on to you now.

Modern music institutions seem to be very concerned about teaching *what is possible* to play. Because of this approach, students leave thinking that they *should* cram as many of these theoretical options as possible into their solos. But the truth is, *the music comes first*. Theory is just a way of explaining what happened afterwards. When I play, I very rarely think about theory. In fact, it only really gets a look in when I'm in a tight spot! Over the years, the musicians I've played with have shown me a few great concepts, but most of my ideas come from mimicking the great players I grew up listening to.

Normally, my soloing ideas are quite simple and begin as *variations* to the melody. I have developed a simple way to target the most important notes in the melody and then build short *motifs* around them. These motifs start simple, then I use my jazz vocabulary and language to embellish them and grow them into fully improvised solos. This not only helps to develop a cohesive solo that tells a story, it helps the audience to understand and engage with what is happening.

The beauty of this approach is not just that it is instant, or that it requires a minimum of theory, it's that the solos you create are tightly linked to the melody and therefore *naturally musical*. I'll say it again, your audience will thank you! They will be able to follow your musical ideas easily and enjoy an improvised performance that relates strongly to the tune they came to hear. Many of them won't know *why* they enjoy your music more than other, more cerebral solos, but they will definitely relate to it more strongly and engage with your solos on a more profound level.

Ultimately, this book is about simplifying your thinking and building beautiful jazz solos. I hope you find it refreshing, but most of all, remember to have fun and enjoy the music!

A Note from Joseph

Once again I can't believe my luck! I'm sitting here writing a book on Jazz guitar with one of my musical heroes. I feel very privileged and honoured to be working with Martin on this book.

This book is the culmination of sitting in Martin's Scottish studio, firing as many awkward questions as I could at him in an eight-hour period. The difficulty for me as a writer is that Martin's virtuosity and fluency on the guitar is very much like the way you and I speak English. When I said to Martin, "Stop!... why did you play that note?!" I may as well have asked him, "Why did you just use the word 'hat'?" His response is, "Well, that's just the right word for the thing on that guy's head!"

For Martin, music is simply another language with words, phrases and vocabulary that is used when appropriate. As such, there's often no theoretical answer to the question, "Why are you playing that?" – it's simply a case of him applying a vocabulary that's been learned, invented and honed over half a decade of playing.

I've spent time around a lot of great guitarists, and out of all of them, Martin's soloing is the closest to someone simply sitting you down and telling you a story. For him, soloing is another form of speaking and is created in much the same way as asking a great novelist to spontaneously write a book. The words and music just flow and create something new and beautiful every time.

That said, I did ask Martin a lot of awkward question and squeezed as much information out of him as I could. There's a definite structure to what he plays and a wonderful logic behind his music. The main emphasis is on *developing the melody* and taking the tune of the music to somewhere new. There's very little reliance on "jazz theory" and he certainly isn't thinking "OK, this is a bar of A minor, I need to play such and such a scale…" Martin's approach is entirely about using the melody as the driving force to build the solo.

Despite Martin's music sounding incredibly complex, his whole approach is to simplify everything. For instance, he doesn't think G7b9b13, he visualises a two-note G Major chord. All the complicated chord extensions can be added later if desired. In addition, Martin knows and *feels* the sound of every chord tone. He understands what *mood* is created by adding a 9th, a b5 or a 13th. It's a very pure, musical approach.

As you can probably already tell, this book is light on theory, but we will discuss concepts like the intervals of a chord, such as the root, 3rd, 5th, 7th and 9th. If you're not familiar with these terms then you would probably benefit from doing some preparatory work before diving in. May I humbly suggest my book **Chord Tone Soloing for Jazz Guitar** as it will quickly get you soloing and develop your understanding of these essential elements of music.

So, if not "formal jazz theory", then what are you going to learn from this book?

The first thing is that it will grow your jazz vocabulary massively. There are hundreds of notated examples of Martin's playing that give logical insight into how to actually build a musical jazz guitar solo. We'll begin by learning how to vary a tune's melody to inspire and structure your solo, then teach you how to develop your improvisation just as a master jazz guitarist would do.

You'll discover how to break down the harmony of a jazz tune into its simplest elements and use it as a framework to underpin your creativity.

You'll study how Martin develops a musical jazz solo in real time, using an unexpected melody that you already know.

You will understand and master great phrasing and how to "swing" on your guitar

You'll discover how to create interest in your playing and, finally, piece it all together with transcribed etudes of Martin's solos.

This is the most practical, musical and above all hands-on jazz guitar book I've ever written and I'm very proud to be a part of it. All the answers to how to play jazz guitar are here.

Oh, and we talk about musical colours quite lot, and we're English so we spell it with a U!

Get the Audio

The audio files for this book are available to download for free from **www.fundamental-changes.com.** The link is in the top right-hand corner. Click on the "Guitar" link then simply select this book title from the drop-down menu and follow the instructions to get the audio.

We recommend that you download the files directly to your computer, not to your tablet, and extract them there before adding them to your media library. You can then put them onto your tablet, iPod or burn them to CD. On the download page there are instructions and we also provide technical support via the contact form.

For over 350 Free Guitar Lessons with Videos Check out:

www.fundamental-changes.com

Over 10,000 fans on Facebook: **FundamentalChangesInGuitar**

Tag us for a share on Instagram: **FundamentalChanges**

Get the Video

As a special bonus to buyers of this book, Martin Taylor has two videos that explain every key element of his walking bass and chords technique, that are not available anywhere else. Follow this link to view/download the content:

https://fundamental-changes.teachable.com/p/single-note/

Or use the short link:

https://geni.us/singlenote

If you type above link into a browser, please note that there is no "www."

You can also scan the QR code below to view the videos on your smartphone:

Chapter One – Melody and Variation

Throughout my years of teaching I have noticed that many guitarists struggle with jazz improvisation. Often, excellent guitarists who are well-versed in rock and blues will come to me for jazz lessons. When I ask them to play a jazz tune and take a solo, however, they often clam up and start "playing theory" as soon as the solo begins. When I ask them what they're thinking about when they play, their answer is often along the lines of:

"Well, that's a minor II chord, so I need to play a Dorian scale on that. Then the V chord moves to a minor I chord, which means I need to play the Altered scale there. To do that, I used a substitution and played a Maj7#5 arpeggio built from the #9 before resolving to the Lydian mode on the tonic chord."

I get anxious just typing that, never mind trying to play it!

It all sounds very academic and clever, but almost without exception, when students think like this during their solos, they don't sound great. When the melody stops and the solo starts, you can *hear them playing theory*. What's worse is that any sense of melody disappears as they try to "chase the chord changes" in their solo.

In this chapter, I want to offer you a better way – an older method of jazz soloing that is easier, sounds better, is more relatable to your audience, and will simplify your whole approach to playing. This is the *traditional* way to build a jazz solo and is a more authentic, musical way to approach the art. Just like most secrets, once the smoke and mirrors are removed, you'll see that it's really quite simple to get started.

The truth is, all the great musicians you've listened to and admire, who can play astonishingly advanced music, have all been through (and continue to work on) the process I'm about to teach you. Their cutting edge theory is built on these solid foundations. That's why they sound great. It's not advanced theory that makes a fantastic player, it's developing a jazz language based around the melody of the tune.

This is the first step of your new jazz soloing journey, because what I'm about to share with you will show you what jazz musicians *actually* do when they improvise. Are you ready?

Secret Number One: Replace the word "improvisation" with the word *variation*.

Being forced to "improvise" immediately puts pressure on you. It describes the daunting task of having to create great music from nothing, in real time, in front of an audience. What a terrifying prospect!

I promise you that I don't get struck by a lightning bolt of inspiration every time I solo. Instead, I begin every solo by playing *small variations to the melody* of the tune.

Think about this for a minute.

The melody is the strongest part of the tune. You don't leave a concert humming the chord progression! Almost all jazz standards were originally vocal songs, which is why they have such strong, memorable tunes. This means you can create a strong, meaningful solo by staying close to the melody and adding small variations. Even if the audience don't understand what's going on musically, they'll feel that your variations are related to the melody they've just heard. It will be a strong, tangible experience for them.

If you solo by varying the melody, you not only bring your audience along for the ride, you also have ready-made melodic material you can develop naturally – you're not starting from scratch.

Not only that, soloing by varying the melody gives you an entire *structure* and *framework* for your solo to exist in. You'll never get "lost in the chord changes" and, most importantly, you won't have to magically create a whole new musical theme on the spot.

By thinking of "melodic variation" rather than "improvisation", you get melodic ideas for free and you give your solo a meaningful structure.

The secret to strong jazz soloing is to learn how to vary a melody and develop it. Once you can do this, everything else falls into place.

Let's begin to learn how to vary a simple melody I've composed over a set of very familiar chord changes. You may recognise this melody from my previous book, **Beyond Chord Melody**.

The chord changes can be played on guitar like this:

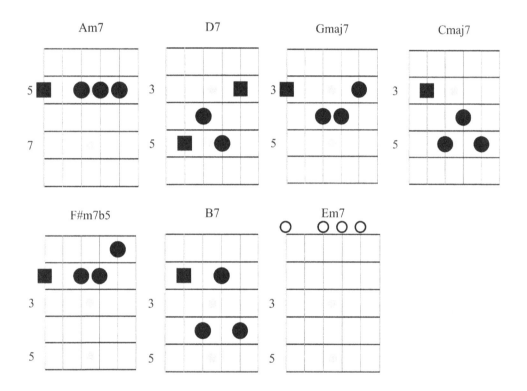

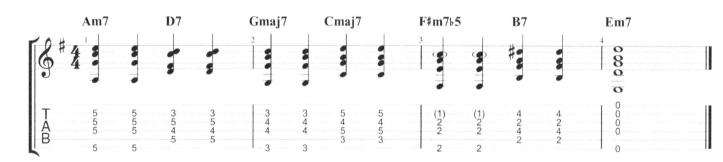

Memorise the position of each chord because this will form a geographic structure for your variations – something we'll discuss in greater detail later.

Now learn and memorise the tune that'll be the workhorse for the rest of this chapter.

Example 1a

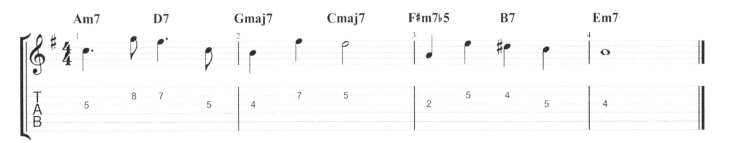

When you're comfortable playing the melody over the chord changes from memory, play it through again and really pay attention to which notes you feel are the strongest and most important in the phrase. To my ears, the most important notes in this melody are the ones that fall on the first beat of each chord. I call these "hit points" – they are essential in defining the shape of the melody.

Learn them now in this reduced version of the melody. Notice that I've added the bass note for each chord. First play the hit point notes on their own, then add in the bass note below them so you can hear and locate them in the context of the chord.

Example 1b

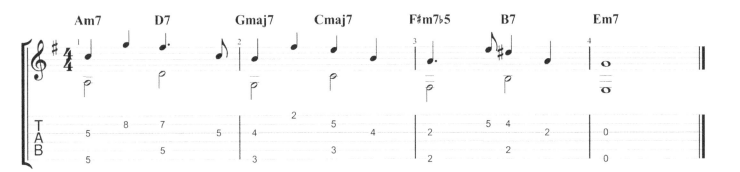

When the hit points are strong in your mind, go back and play the full melody a few times to hear how the hit points relate to the tune. When you're confident, it's time to start adding a little variation to the tune.

As mentioned, very often improvisation is taught in a way that says, "You can play this scale over this chord…" but this is too far removed from what actually happens when jazz musicians start improvising. The more intuitive, melodic approach is to *vary the melody* and that's what we'll do now. Learn the following variation to the melody, then compare it to the hit points in the previous example.

Example 1c

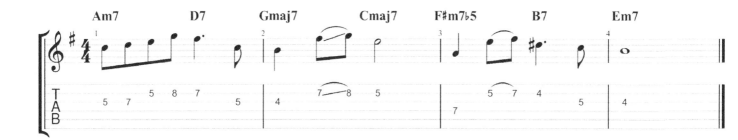

What am I thinking when I create little variations like this?

The first thing is that I keep those hit points strong in my ears. Each short variation I play is aiming for the next hit point in the sequence. In the previous example, I began on a hit point, then added a variation that led to the next one, then repeated this structure throughout. You don't have to begin on a hit point (and we will look at that in more detail later), but for now, beginning on a strong melody note will really help to anchor your variations to the melody.

The next thing to understand is that all these variations tend to fall quite nicely under the fingers when I play the root notes shown in Example 1b. These root notes help me "map" out the fretboard and I have lots vocabulary in each position. These days everything I play is led by my ears, but they have been trained by years of listening, copying, experimenting and playing – just like how you learned to speak English.

The bass notes and melodic hit points are like an early pencil sketch of an oil painting. Once I have the sketch in place, I gradually fill in the colour. By seeing the chord structure and melody like this, I am stripping the tune right down to its basics. I can then find different ways of moving between each hit point while keeping the chord structures in mind.

Play the hit points from Example 1b again, then try this new variation. The bass notes are shown in brackets. Don't play them at first, just learn the melody.

Example 1d

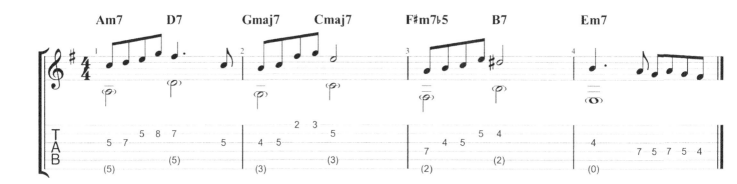

When you're ready, try playing Example 1d again, but add in the bass notes on each chord.

Remember, the bass notes and melodic hit points are an early sketch of the finished painting. I also visualise a simplified version of the chord structure in my mind when I play. I do this by adding the 3rd (or 10th) of the chord on one of the middle strings. The 3rd of a chord tells us whether it has a major or minor quality and is incredibly useful for guiding our ears. Most of the time when it comes to chords, especially when I'm improvising, all I think about is the root and 3rd. They are the bare minimum needed to define the harmony and once they are in place, we can add the different colours of extensions and alterations as we wish.

I love this approach because instead of thinking about how to play over complicated chords like B7#9b13, I'm really just thinking about the root and 3rd.

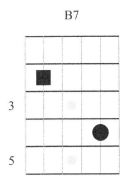

B7

I don't have complicated harmony going on in my mind, I just have this simple outline of each chord shape. Anything that sounds complicated in my solos comes from variations to the melody that are built around the root and 3rd (tenth) shape.

Play through the "root and 10th" chords of our tune.

Example 1e

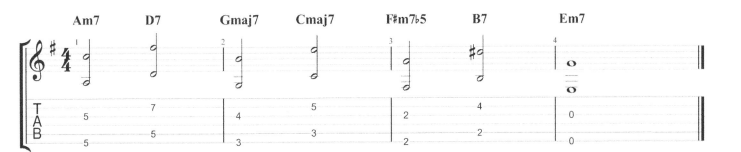

It just so happens that the melody of our tune is built around the 10ths of the chord. You can probably already hear this in the previous example, but of course this won't always be the case.

This reduced sketch of the song's harmony means that we are not keeping too much information in mind while we use melodic variations to colour-in the melody. Instead of thinking in terms of complex chords, we are reducing them down to simplify our thinking. We can add the other colours later.

These 10th structures are easy to move around the neck and they're also very recognisable to us. Our tune is in the key of E Minor, so learn the root and tenth voicings up and down the E string and A string.

Example 1f

Now we have the neck mapped out in root and 10th chords, let's return to our melody and look at some more variations we could create. If you are new to this, there are a couple of common *approach note* patterns you should know. The first begins an 1/8th note before the beat and approaches the target note from a scale tone below.

Example 1g

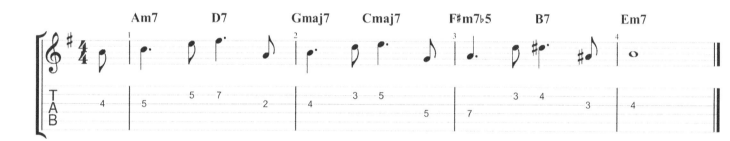

The next begins a beat before the target note and approaches the target note from the scale tone below, then the scale tone above.

Example 1h

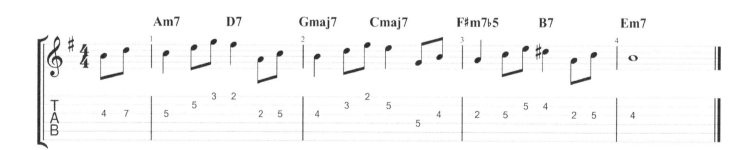

When you have got these ideas under your fingers it's worthwhile practising these approach notes patterns on the root, 3rd, 5th and 7th of each chord as it will help train your ears to hear some strong melodic shapes. For a complete guide to this technique, check out Joseph's book, **Chord Tone Soloing for Jazz Guitar.**

Let's begin to create some simple variations to our melodic hit points by approaching each target note from a scale tone above. It's a simple idea, but you'll quickly start to hear some new melodic variation possibilities.

Example 1i

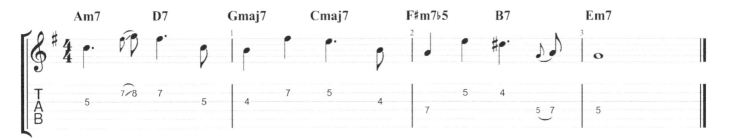

Now here's a slightly longer phrase that targets the hit points.

Example 1j

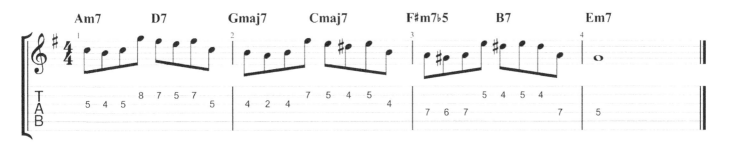

Next, we can introduce some rhythmic variation.

Example 1k

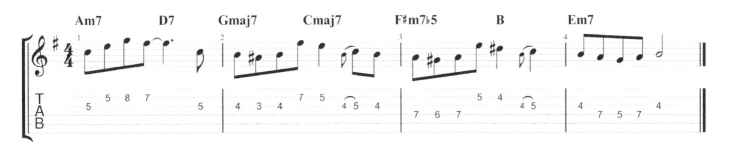

So far, all these variations have used scale notes (from the E Harmonic Minor scale if you need to know!) but of course, jazz musicians love to use chromatic notes to link up the hit points in the melody too. A chromatic note is any note that doesn't exist in the scale, so when you start to understand how they work, *every* note in music becomes available! Don't panic though… we're just adding a few more variations to the melody.

Example 1l

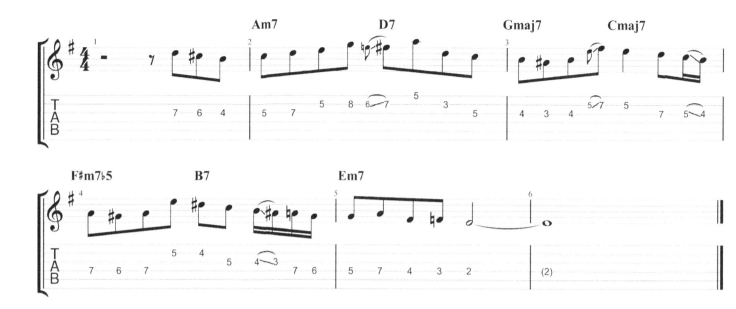

Here's another chromatic idea. Can you hear how the melody has influenced the line, but the simple addition of a few chromatic notes starts to make this sound quite jazzy?

Example 1m

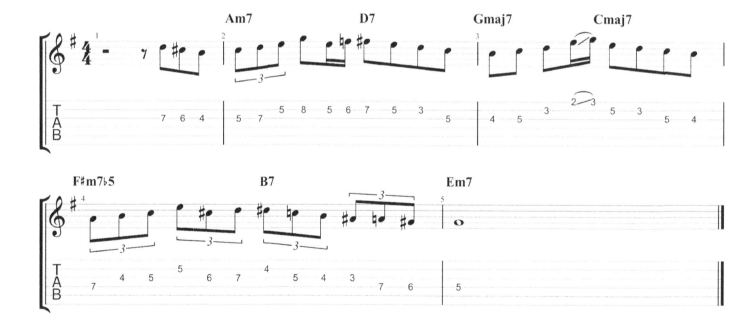

Playing with chromatic ideas is a lot of fun! Here's another longer idea, played in free time, that continues to target the hit points of the melody.

Example 1n

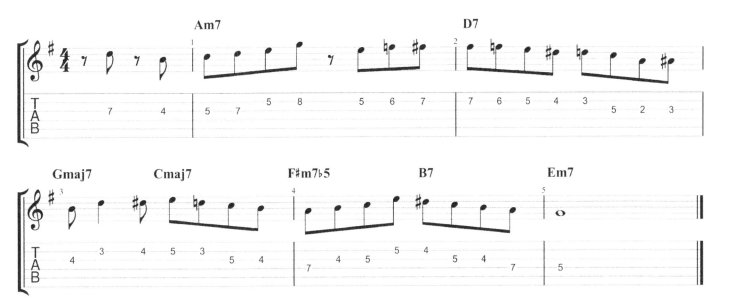

Now it's over to you for a while, to spend some time exploring different ways to approach the hit points of the melody using scale notes and chromatics. The best way to learn this is to listen to great musicians playing and recycle their ideas (I always joke with my students that we're helping the planet by recycling!) These approaches are used all the time and now you know what you're listening for, it should be easier to pick them out. Even if you don't copy their idea perfectly, listening to how other musicians approach this will help you understand the melodic shapes and rhythmic possibilities you can use.

As you get better at decorating the melodic hit points, you might stumble on an idea you really like. When you hit upon a variation, you can develop it into a *motif* – an idea that can be transferred around the chord changes and adapted as necessary to develop it into something new. For example, here's a little melody I came up with based around a trill. Notice how I take it around the chords and change it up slightly at the end.

Example 1o

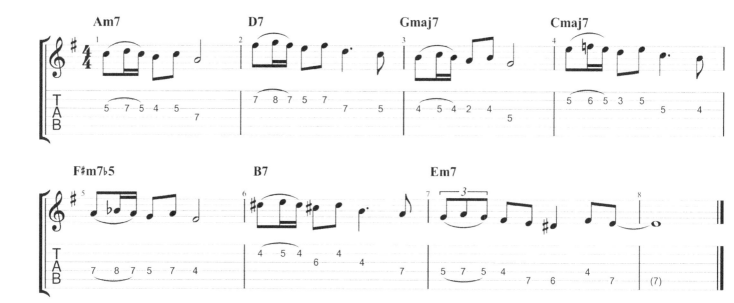

Here's another motif that I could take around the chord sequence. Again, you can hear how it starts early and targets the hit points of the melody

Example 1p

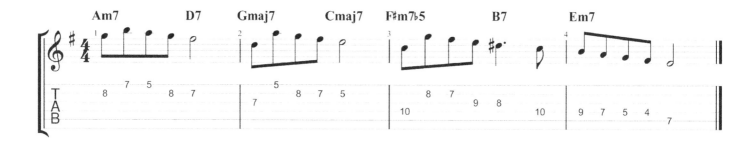

As you get more confident, you can begin to move away from the hit points of the original melody and create new motifs around your own hit points. This will happen naturally as you spend time practising. While these hit points will probably be arpeggio notes of the chords, they don't have to be, in which case the possibilities become endless. The only thing limiting you right now is your vocabulary of ideas. The secret is to listen to as much music as possible and steal the little motifs that stand out to you, then immediately use them in your playing.

Example 1q

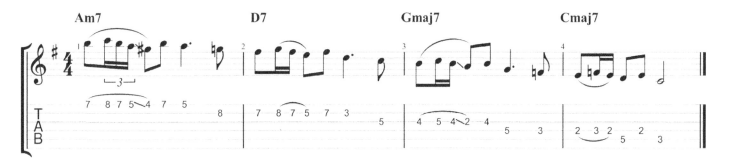

As good as it is to practice a single motif around the whole chord progression, it's more musical to *develop* it as your solo progresses. This could begin as simply as practising different motifs on each chord, but when you've learnt enough musical ideas you'll begin to organically develop them on the fly. The next example is more of a free idea that begins by targeting a hit point but then grows into a more musical phrase.

Example 1r

Here's a longer idea that develops quickly. It's a more advanced idea, but break it down and play it slowly to understand how I target the strong notes of the melody. You might want to learn small fractions of this idea at first and explore them individually.

Example 1s

The next stage is to introduce some gaps in your variations and begin to think in phrases, just as you would when talking. This next example is split into clear phrases based around each pair of chords. Notice that I've stopped limiting myself to the hit points of the melody. This is a natural stage as your variations develop and means that you're beginning to trust your ears.

Example 1t

The next idea goes a little further out again and introduces more chromatic notes for you to play with and learn from. I played it freely and you'll probably hear me making comments as I play!

Example 1u

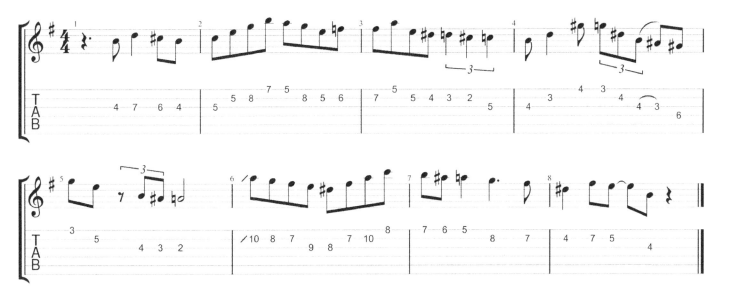

Finally, here's a fairly diatonic idea that really develops the line and is a long way from the original target notes of the melody. However, because the music developed naturally and your audience were brought here in simple logical steps, it is still a strong melodic idea.

Example 1v

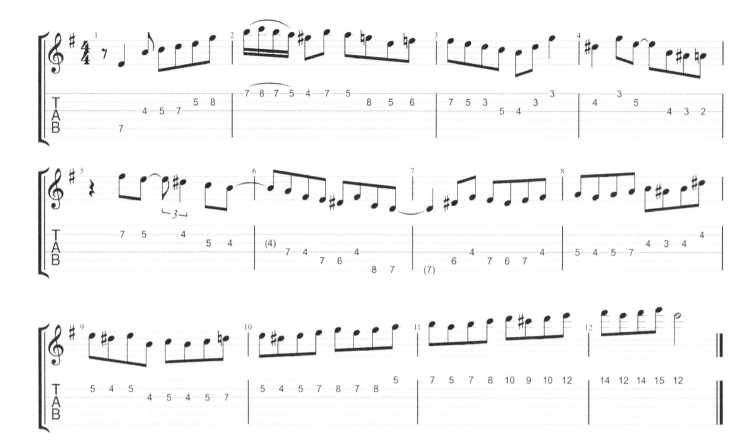

It's time to move on, but it's important to say that what you've learnt here is a massive part of the puzzle when it comes to creating well-conceived, improvised jazz lines. The solos of the greatest guitar players all retain a strong connection to the melody. There is a process to this:

- Learn the melody

- Define the hit points

- Vary the melody around the hit points

- Build motifs and decorations around the hit points

- Create your own hit points

- Build on these and develop them

Think of your improvisation as storytelling. Your strong connection to the melody (or main theme of the story) will take your audience with you.

Chapter Two – Other Target Notes and Colour Tones

In the previous chapter, we began our journey of melodic variation by creating hit points based on the melody, which was based on 3rd intervals. But what if the melody was built around 9ths or 5ths or 13ths? In this chapter we'll discuss the idea that it's not just chord tones that can form hit points for our solos. In fact, we can target pretty much any note we want on any chord to add colour and depth to the music.

As we saw at the end of the previous chapter, as we improvise variations on the melody, we naturally begin to target different notes related to each chord. And each of these notes has a different "colour" and adds a different mood to your solo.

There are no rules for how quickly you introduce these other colours. You might want to introduce 9ths and 13ths straight away, or maybe you want to stick to targeting "safer" chord tones when you first begin to vary the melody. The only way to judge what works is to develop your ears, and the only way to do that is to do a lot of listening, practice and *playing*!

I've been doing this professionally for 50 years, so I've experienced a lot of music. My ears are the boss now and I play 9ths, 11ths, 13ths and other intervals without really thinking about them consciously – my fingers simply play what I hear in my head.

That said, in this chapter I'll give you many starting points for your explorations of musical colour and hopefully set you on a path to your own sonic discovery.

Let's quickly recap the melody and hit points of the tune, which happens to be based on 3rds.

Example 2a

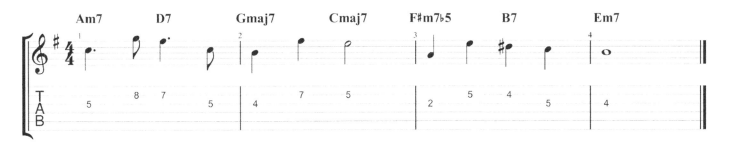

We also learnt that we can embellish those hit points by adding little variations around the melody, as in Example 2b.

Example 2b

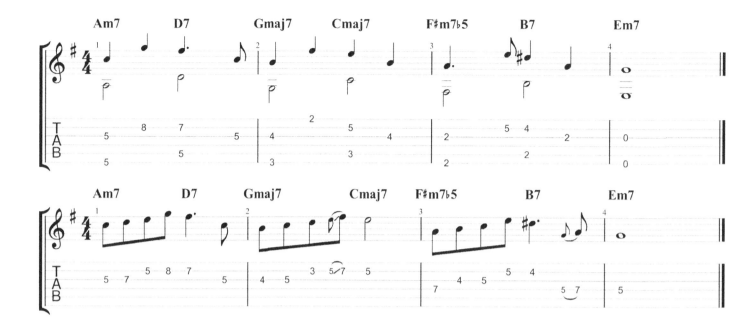

Instead of targeting the melody note (in this case the 3rd), however, I could target the 5th of each chord. The 5ths are located here. (Notice that I'm reducing down the complex F#m7b5 chord to simply an "F minor" sound).

Example 2c

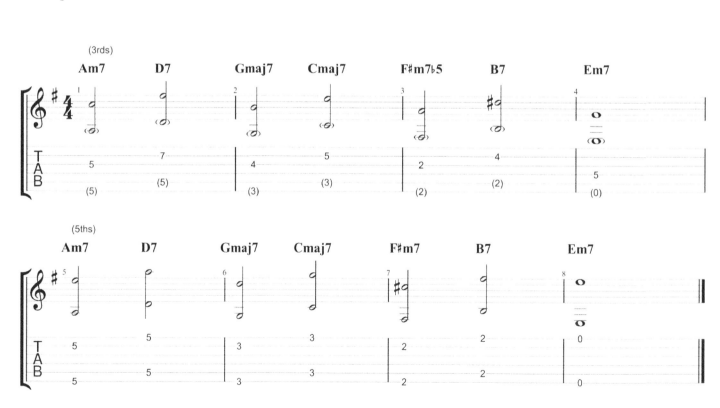

Once we have located the 5th interval of each chord, we can play a little motif that targets them. (In this example, I finish on the *root* of the final E minor chord to resolve the line, because that's where my ears take me).

Example 2d

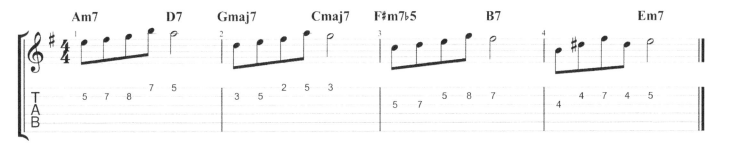

Now it's your turn. I want you to come up with five different ways to approach the 5th of each chord. Remember, you can use scale notes and chromatic ideas. Refer to the previous chapter and see how I targeted the 3rd to give you some ideas. Don't worry about playing the "correct" scale. You've used all these notes before in Chapter One. Your ears will tell you if there's a sound in there that you don't like.

Next, try combining ideas so that sometimes you target the 5th and sometimes the 3rd.

This line begins on the 3rd of Am then targets the 5th of D and continues alternating the target notes throughout the phrase.

Example 2e

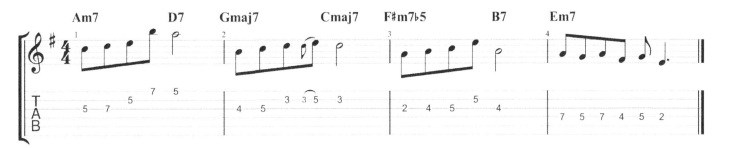

When you can confidently target both the 5th and the 3rd you're really cooking with gas! Put down the book for a while and begin freely targeting whichever note you feel like in your melody variations. You can use the original shape of the tune to help you, or just see where your ears take you.

This is a great time to simply have fun and explore the guitar. Do you see now why establishing the geography of the chord shapes is so important? All these phrases just begin to fall under your fingers as you learn where the strong target notes are in the relation to the chord.

Now go and invent five short melodies that target the root of each chord, and five that target the 7th. You already know where the root of each chord is, so here is a chart showing the location of the 7ths.

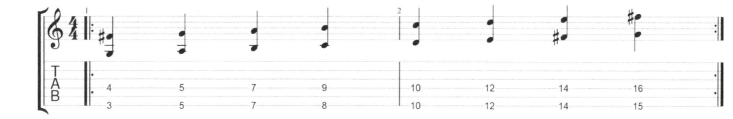

7ths are harder to hear at first but are an important note to know in each chord.

There are always new melodic ideas to discover. It's a lifelong pursuit, but if you listen to a lot of jazz you will quickly start to recognise and use these melodies in your own playing.

Spend time now combining lines that target whichever chord tone notes you feel like (1, 3, 5 or 7). Be aware that becoming fluent at this will take time. It's a slow process but don't be discouraged. You'll gradually begin to hear the phrases form under your fingers. To begin with, include the root note of each chord, so you can hear the effect of the other notes you're targeting.

In addition to the chord tones of the triad (1, 3 and 5) and the 7th, the 9th is a beautiful colour to target. It adds a richness and lightness to the chord. In Example 2f, I hold down just the root, 7th and the 9th of each chord, then play a simple motif that bounces between the 9th and root on the sixth-string. The chords are A minor, G Major and F# minor.

Example 2f

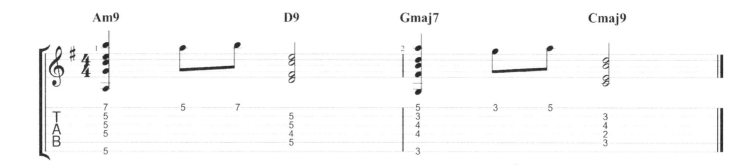

It's not always appropriate to target the 9th on every chord, but it sounds fantastic on the tonic G Major chord.

Example 2g

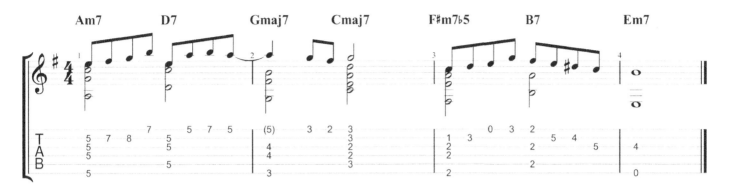

Once you have worked through the process of targeting the chord tones we've discussed so far (1, 3, 5, 7 and 9) and you have your geography figured out, you can mix and match these ideas, targeting the intervals freely. In Example 2h I jump up the neck and target different notes on each chord. However, there's a very important lesson I want you to take away with you here: *the chord position I choose follows the melody I want to play*.

Melody always comes first, so if I hear a jump in the melody, I'll often voice my chord higher on the neck. That's why it's so important to know the root and 10th chord voicings up and down each string.

You can analyse the following line to see which intervals the melody targets on each chord, but also use your ears. Can you pick out the sound and *feeling* of a 9th, a 3rd of a 5th? Hearing these intervals as colours and feeling their moods is so important for your musicality.

Can you see how I use chromatics to link together some of the target notes? These lines aren't composed, this is just me playing what I hear in my head.

Example 2h

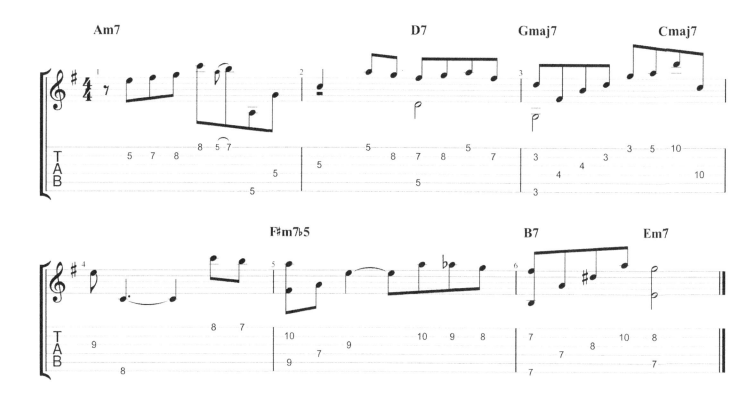

While you're up at the higher end of the guitar, here's a useful line to link together the Am7 and D7 chords.

Example 2i

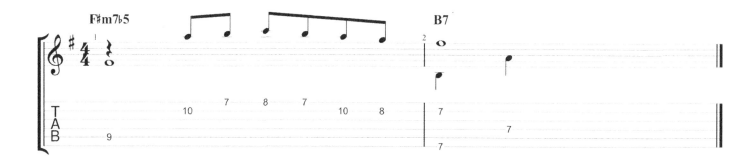

Another lovely warm interval to target on the Gmaj7 chord is the 6th. Here's one way you could do that, but explore your guitar and see how many melodies you can make that end on this note. The 6th sounds like it wants to resolve to the 5th, but it doesn't have to.

Example 2j

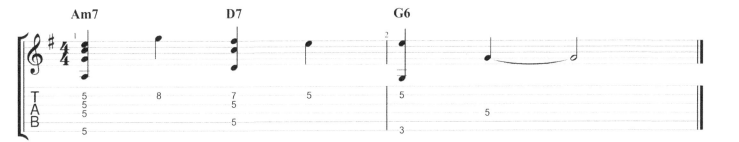

It's important to note that the F#m chord is a little bit different, so instead of playing a 5th here (C#), it actually sounds much better to play a b5 (C). I won't go into the theory behind this now – I just want you to hear the effect of the note, rather than it be an academic exercise. This example teaches you to hear the sound of the b5 in context over the F# bass note. Use your second finger to play the bass note.

Example 2k1

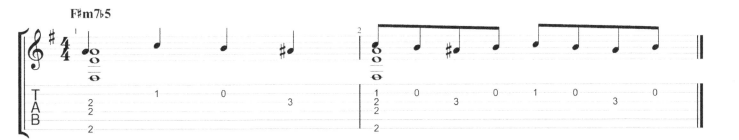

The b5 note really wants to resolve to the 5th on the B7 chord.

Example 2k2

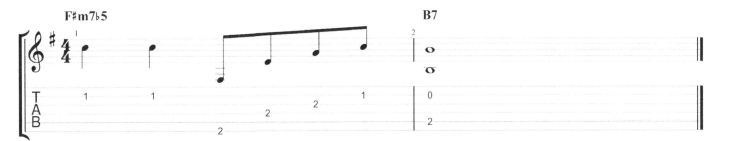

Here's a line that highlights the beauty of the b5 over F#m, resolving to the 5th of B7.

Example 2k3

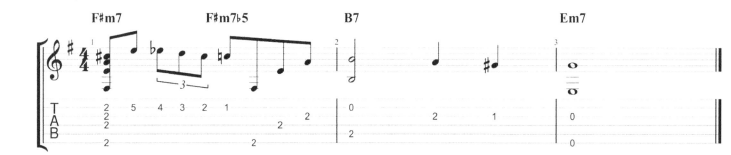

This line is also very pretty and targets mostly 9ths, with a b9 played over the B7 chord.

Example 2l

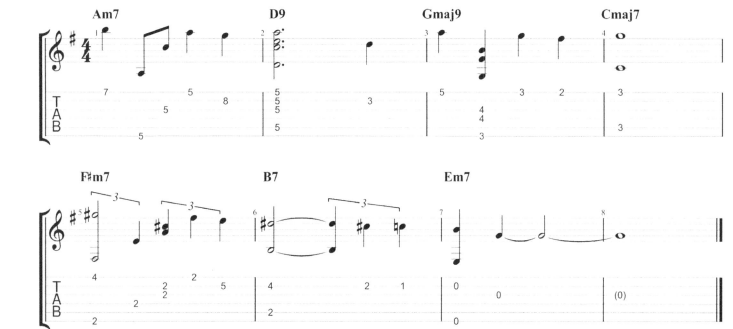

An Important Substitution

Before we move on, I want to talk about a very important chord substitution idea that I often use in my playing. A chord substitution is simply playing one chord instead of another. This means that when we think of a substitution as a chord, we can target its chord tones in our solo, just as we have been doing so far.

I want to keep our discussion about this concept as simple as possible. When we talk about substitutions, students often reach for the theory books and come up with some complex ideas. My way of thinking for chord substitutions (and knowing when to play them) is so easy it can be boiled down to a single sentence:

"You can approach any chord chromatically from a semitone above."

This means that instead of playing the following:

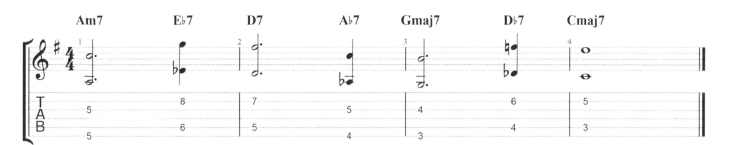

You could play…

The series of bass notes illustrated in the second diagram is just like a walking bassline. We could play all of those substitutions all the time, but the music would start to sound heavy and complicated. Instead, we can pick and choose from them.

Let's explore the possibilities of just one of them – the Db7 chord that precedes Cmaj7.

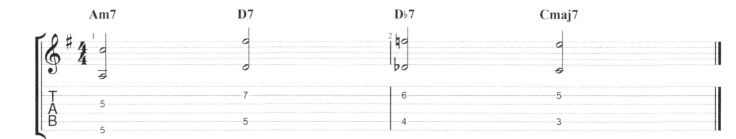

Now we have a Db7 in the first half of bar three, we can use its chord tones (and extensions if you like) as target notes in an improvised melody. The fingering of the following example will take a little bit of getting used to if you've not done this before, but I think it's important and a feature of my style to play the bassline as I play the melody.

Here I play a melody through the unaltered changes, then play the same thing with the Db7 substitution. I've chosen a richer colour here and played a Db9#11. You can hear how using just this point of tension makes the line a lot more interesting.

Example 2m

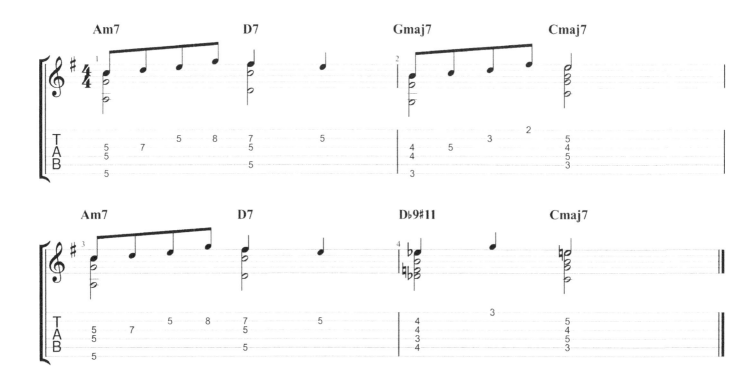

When I play these substitutions I don't really think about a separate scale choice I should be playing over the chord, but here's a line I use a lot that contains a great collection of notes from which you can create a melody.

Example 2n

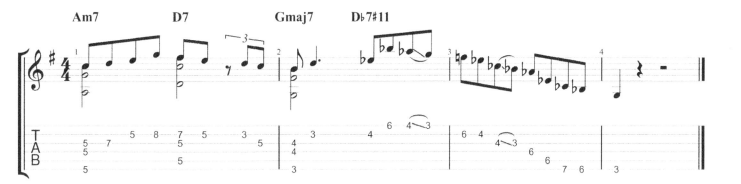

This concept can be applied to any chord you like, but playing it just before the Cmaj7 is a wonderful place to start. Even though you might play just one or two notes on that chord, it adds interest and sophistication to your solo. See how many melodies you can create with the notes of Db7 resolving to a chord tone of the Cmaj7 chord.

Which Colour Should I Use?

So far, we've discussed different ways of targeting the most important notes of each chord and also explored a simple substitution idea. The danger is that we use this information in an almost mathematical fashion, targeting one interval then the next and entirely forgetting that the aim is to create great music! The exercises have been useful to help you locate the chord tones, but want I really want you to focus on is the colours and moods each interval creates against the underlying chords.

How do they make you feel? And which interval should you use when?

I want to take a moment to describe how I think of the different notes in terms of their colour and mood. Like an artist, we have a broad palette of colours to choose from with many different shades – not just black, white and primary colours.

If I play a straight G Major chord it sounds solid, like a primary colour. But if I add the major 7th, now I've got a shade. Suddenly we're on a beach drinking Pina Coladas! It's a pretty sound that always reminds of me *The Girl from Ipanema*, especially when combined with the 9th.

If I lower that to the b7th, it quickly becomes more tense and bluesy.

Lower it again to the 6th and it creates a different feeling all together. What does it mean to you? Play the following example.

Example 2o

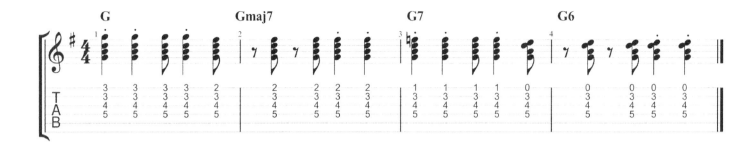

When you think more in terms of what mood you want to create (romantic, wistful, reflective, tense etc) it will affect your choice of melodic hit point. Here I've chosen to target the 9th on the Am chord, the 5th on the D7, and the 7ths on both Gmaj7 and Cmaj7. Notice how I roll my picking fingers through the chords to add another texture to the music.

Example 2p

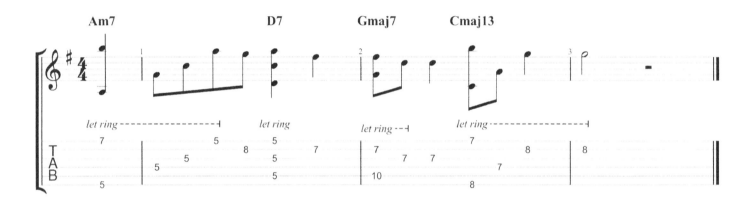

When it comes to deciding which tones to target, it all comes back to colours. Each chord tone or *extension* (9, 11 or 13) represents a different colour to me. Which one I choose depends on what kind of picture I'm painting.

To use a different analogy, it's like cooking. You wouldn't want to use the same ingredients in every meal. Adding chromatic notes is like adding some chili – it's only appropriate for certain dishes! So for example, while we can add the b5, #9 or #5 to any chord, you'll probably find that these work best (to begin with) on the dominant 7 chords.

I've added some spice in Example 2q. This is how the #5 on the B7 chord sounds moving to the 9th on the Em.

Example 2q

Work through the progression, focusing on each chord in turn, and listen to the sound of each tone against the root and 10th voicing. See how each one makes you feel. Internalise the sound.

This is an extremely worthwhile exercise, but a lifetime's work. The context in which you hear the intervals will often be different, so it will take time to absorb the sounds. However, there's nothing wrong with starting now. Listen to the roots, 9ths, 3rds 11ths etc at the top of each chord voicing. Try to take an organised approach. Sometimes you might want to play the bass note with your second finger to help you reach the desired pitch.

As you get better at choosing the notes that reflect the mood you're trying to convey, the next stage is to write lines that link them together. We looked at lots of lines that linked chord tones earlier in the chapter, but just for a bit of inspiration here's one that really pushes the boat out.

Let's say you're approaching the Am7 chord and the next note you want to target the b3rd of the D7 chord. Here's a creative line that links them together. It starts a beat before the Am7 and descends chromatically to target the b3 before jumping down a 6th and continuing. This line is a staple bebop idea, so get this important jazz lick in your ears and then try copying the shape beginning from the b3rd of the D7 to target the 3rd of the Gmaj7 chord.

Example 2r

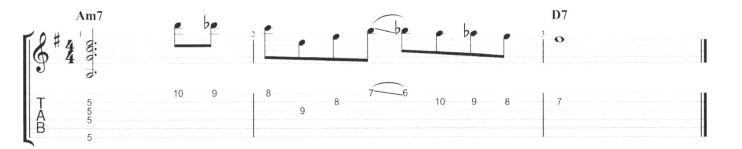

To close this chapter, I want to leave you with a short etude to study that combines many of the ideas we've discussed. Learn it then break it down to see how it links the chord changes together. You can analyse it if you like, but before you do that, I want you to listen to how the target notes make you feel.

The etude begins with me playing the melody to get the sound of the tune into your head, but immediately jumps into quite an intricate solo that misses out many of the variation and development steps I'd normally do. We've covered those – here I want to present a glimpse of where you can take the concept.

You should be able to hear that many of the hit points of the melody are surrounded by free improvisation that consolidates the ideas I've shown you so far.

Example 2s

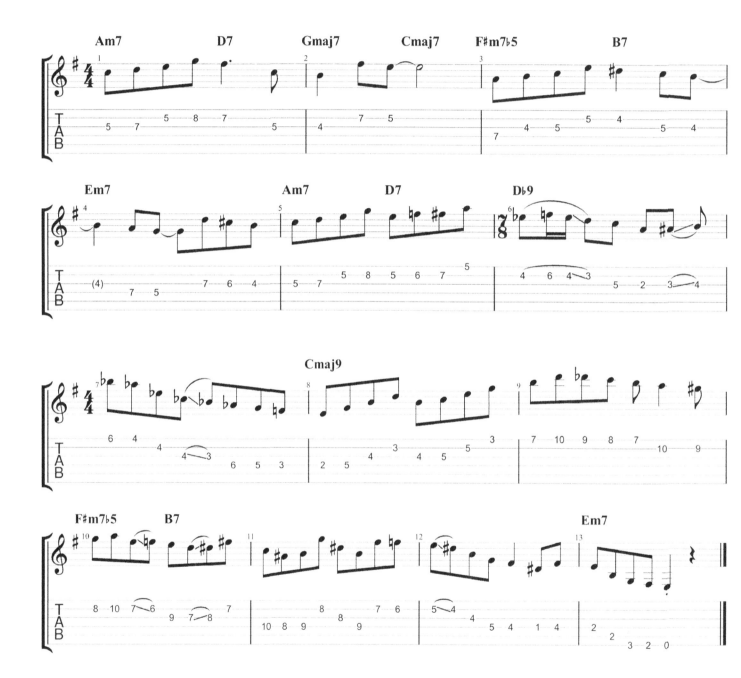

In the next chapter, I'm going to break down layer by layer how it's possible to vary, develop and build a solo on even the most basic of melodies. I think you'll like it!

Chapter Three – Baa Baa Black Sheep

In the previous two chapters, we've laid a lot of the groundwork for meaningful single note soloing, and I've shown you a great deal about varying the melody and targeting chord tones to build a solo. All this was done within the framework of a jazzy chord sequence and we looked at how playing different intervals on those chords affected the colour and mood of your solo.

In this chapter I want to show you just how effective *variation* can be in transforming even the most pedestrian of melodies into a jazz solo that has momentum and tells a story. I've often used this example in my guitar retreats, and it works because *everyone* knows this melody, even if they're not into jazz.

Baa Baa Black Sheep has a strong, simple melody based on the major scale. Because the chord sequence is not remotely jazzy, practising with this tune allows us to forget about the changes and concentrate on learning to develop variations. The goal here is to embellish the tune and build into a creative solo.

We will begin very simply and gradually expand the complexity of the variations until we're playing an exciting solo. You might think that this would result in the melody becoming unrecognisable, but when we underpin the improvisation with our new-found secret strategy of targeting melodic hit points, we will always retain a strong musical link to the melody. What's more, because we begin with simple variations, we can take the listener on a journey so they can hear, step by step, how the solo develops.

This chapter will teach you the art of melodic variation that goes back to the great classical composers like Bach, Mozart and Paganini. Despite our jazz phrasing and chromatic ideas, it's very easy to see how what we do as improvisers builds on the genius of the old masters.

Let's get started.

This chapter doesn't contain a lot of words as I want the music to speak for itself. If you don't already know it (though I doubt it!) here's the melody for *Baa Baa Black Sheep*.

Example 3a

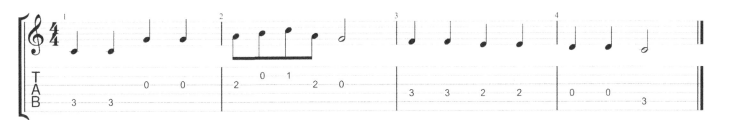

Hopefully it's pretty clear to you already which are the strong target notes of the melody, but I've highlighted the relevant words in the lyrics below, in case you're in any doubt.

Baa baa **black** sheep,

Have you any **wool**?

Yes sir, **yes** sir,

Three bags **full**.

All these notes are contained in the G Major triad, except for the F on the first "yes", which is the 4th.

Let's begin by adding a little motif to the melody to fancy it up a little bit! Notice how the hit points are the same. I just play a slightly different phrase to get to the next hit point.

Example 3b

Here's another little variation.

Example 3c

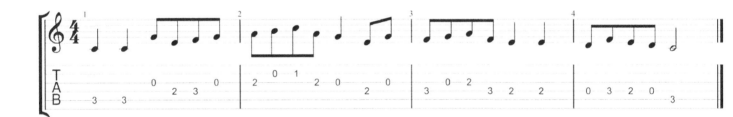

Here's another. I know I have to get to my target note, but how I get there is up to me.

Example 3d

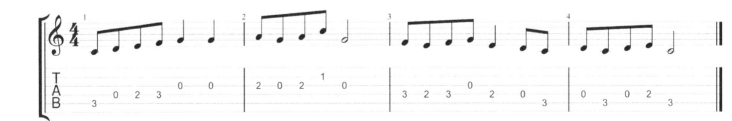

OK, let's get a little more jazzy and use a motif with a little chromaticism.

Example 3e

Example 3f is an idea that disguises the basic melody a little more, but it's definitely still in there.

Example 3f

I've filled in some gaps in the next idea.

Example 3g

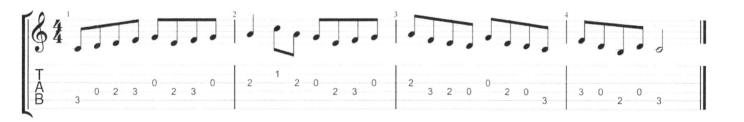

Playing with a different feel can have a dramatic effect on the overall effect of the music, so let's add a bit of swing!

Example 3h

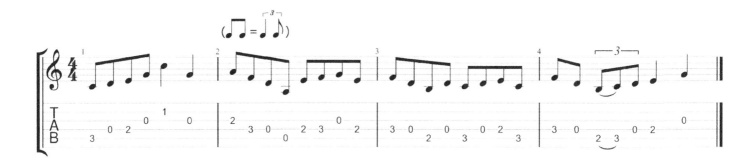

Sometimes it's easier to get a jazz feel without using the open strings. In the next example I take the melody up an octave then add some jazzy embellishments.

Example 3i

Here's a jazz/blues approach to varying the melody. Notice how my *feel* has changed. The notes aren't ringing out as much and I vary my articulation.

Example 3j

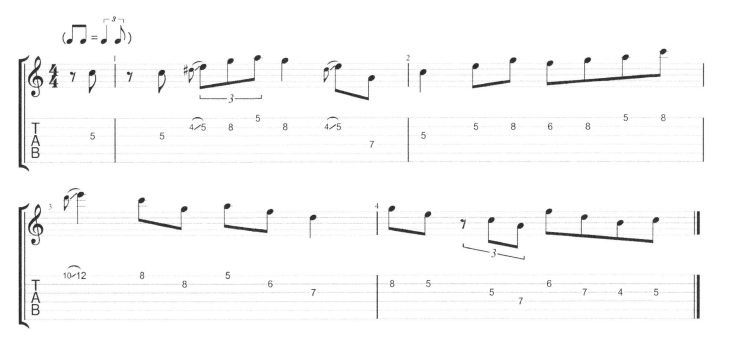

Now I really begin to pull out all the stops. There are chromatics, jazzy motifs and even the Blues scale creeping into my playing here… but you can still hear *Baa Baa Black Sheep* because I've led you to this point in simple steps and I still target the odd hit point.

Example 3k

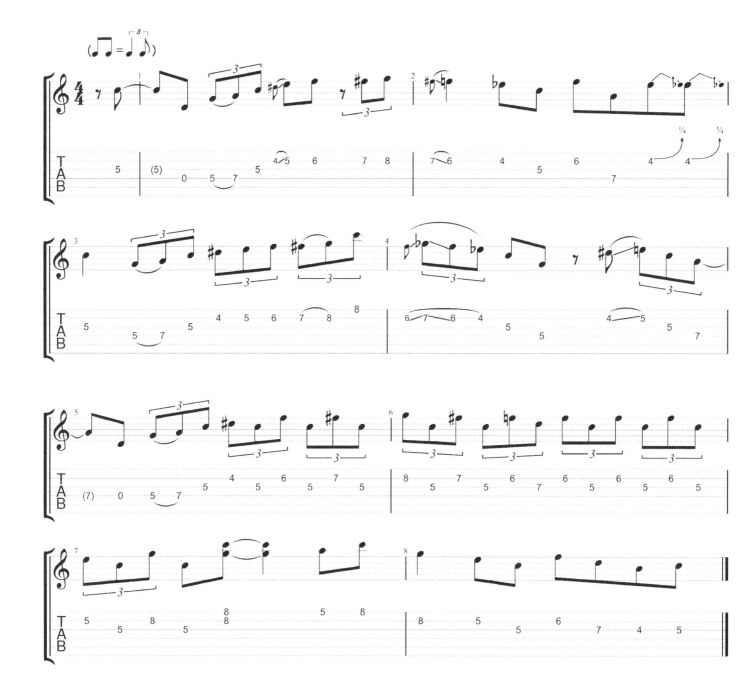

Now we're starting to take a few more liberties with the melody and things are sounding distinctly jazzy. I go twice round the tune here and keep building the variations.

Example 3l

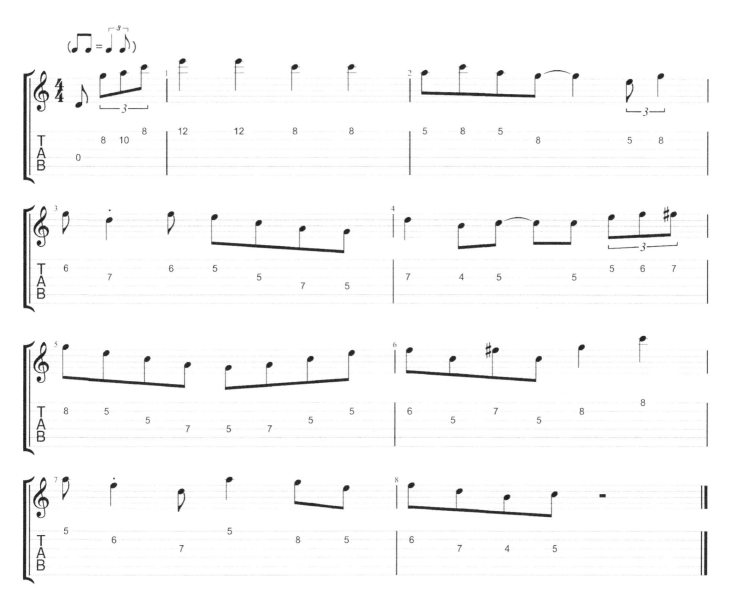

The next line begins sticking closely to the melody and introduces an important jazz pedal note idea that you should learn.

Example 3m

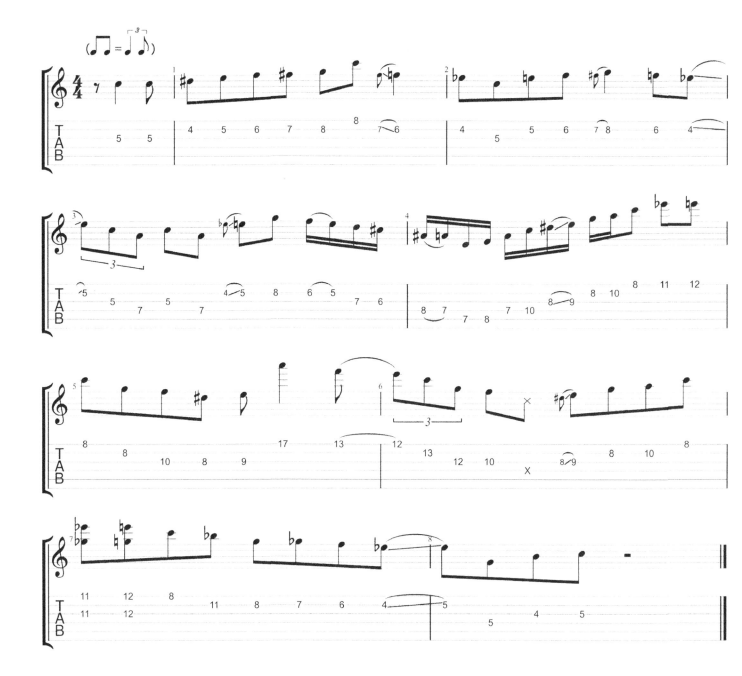

By now, the original melody has been developed so much that I can really play whatever I want. The only hit point in the next example is really the final note of the melody. I've gone "full blues", adding double stops and even a few bends.

Example 3n

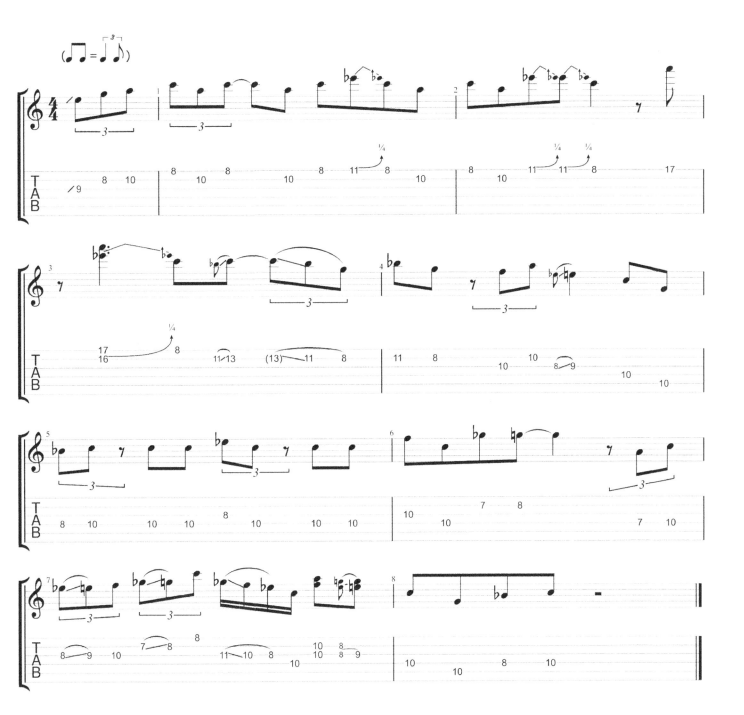

As you practise this approach more and more, some of your ideas will become licks you'll keep and reuse. This is how you'll develop your own language. Here's one final idea. A different take that really articulates the melody and sounds like an authentic early swing lick.

Example 3o

So there you have it: *Baa Baa Black Sheep!* Throughout all those variations I never deviated from the simple chords that underpin the melody. Even when the solo was getting quite advanced, I kept returning occasionally to reference the hit points, and so never lost sight of the melodic structure and strength of the tune.

When you first begin to learn this approach you might find it quite a challenge to come up with new ideas to vary the melody, so I recommend you learn my variations first and steal those ideas to use in your playing. It can be easy to lose the melody of any tune – even one you know inside out – so try humming the hit points as you play to keep in mind the notes you're aiming for. Gradually, your confidence will build and you'll be able to take more liberties with the rhythm and use fewer hit points to give you more freedom.

Don't forget, the secret is to use small variations that take the melody somewhere new. If you can do this, your audience with be right there with you. As you improve this skill, you will naturally become able to start your solos with more intricate variations and jazzier improvisations. Your only goal right now is to see how many ways you can find to vary the melody.

Chapter Four – Developing Vocabulary and Phrasing

After all the work developing your variations in the previous chapters, you might be starting to realise that successfully developing a melody depends on a few things.

First of all, you can create whatever melody you like as long as it is strong and reaches the target note at the right time.

Secondly, the more "connecting" vocabulary you have at your disposal, the more interesting your improvised lines become.

Thirdly, we all have the same twelve notes available to us, it's just how and when we play them that makes us different as soloists!

In this chapter, we will work to develop your vocabulary and get you thinking creatively about phrasing. This isn't a chapter about jazz guitar licks, it's about developing your own musical language on the guitar, which will begin to form your own unique voice.

How do we learn a language? Simple! We copy it from our parents and teachers before adapting it and learning to use it freely to express ourselves.

First, let me make one quick observation. There is a difference between "licks" and "vocabulary".

A lick is generally set in stone. It's a musical phrase that is always played in the same way and probably fits over a specific part of a chord progression. We all have our favourite licks, but they can be limited in their use. Licks are the equivalent of a phrase book when you're visiting a foreign country and don't speak the language well. You can pull out these stock phrases and read them aloud to achieve a desired but specific result.

Having *vocabulary* is different. Vocabulary is an understanding of the language, knowing the meaning of each individual word. Vocabulary is learned through study and immersion in a culture. If licks are a phrase book, vocabulary is an understanding of the how the language is constructed – the grammar and subtle nuances that are at your command when you've truly mastered the language. It's like knowing every available word in the dictionary and being able to combine them in any way you want.

You can, of course, learn vocabulary through learning licks – and this is the best way to begin – but ultimately, isn't it more creative and artistic to create licks that are personal to you through understanding the language?

In this chapter, I'm going to teach you some of my jazz language and you're going to learn it by copying my playing. As you begin to develop your own vocabulary (by using my ideas and taking them in other directions) you'll be able to use that language to connect the hit points in any tune you play.

One of the reasons that my style of guitar playing is very distinctive is that my vocabulary doesn't really come from jazz guitarists. I have always listened to a lot of pianists and horn players. That's nothing new, Django Reinhardt's favourite musician was Louis Armstrong. In fact, one of the challenges that jazz guitarists face is that the language of jazz was developed on horns and saxophones – and these lines are quite difficult to translate onto guitar. This is one of the things you first realise when you learn to play jazz on guitar – nothing really falls under the fingers.

However, it really is essential that you study vocabulary played on the traditional jazz instruments like trumpet, clarinet and saxophone if you want to develop an authentic jazz language. It's a little awkward at first, but you soon get used to the patterns involved.

Here's the sort of line that Django might have played, inspired by a trumpet. Imagine this being played by a trumpet and you'll hear what I mean.

Example 4a

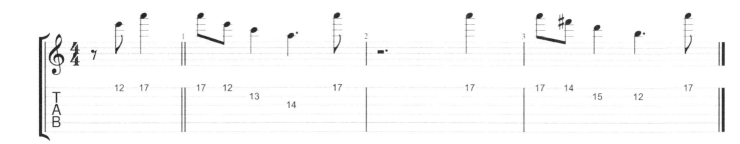

Here's another piece of Django vocabulary, this one inspired by a bugle call. Listen carefully to how I articulate the phrase because I'm copying the way a brass instrument would play it. This line jumps around the neck perhaps more than you'd like, but that's just part of the language. Don't learn this as a lick necessarily, just focus on the articulation and the shape of the line and see if you can use it as a variation to a melody.

Example 4b

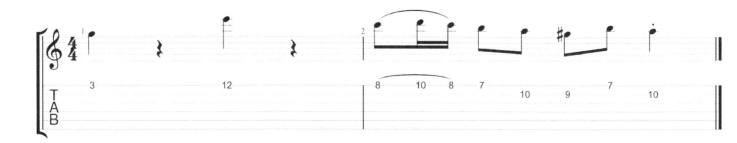

Here's another line that you could imagine Louis Armstrong playing. Again, pay particular attention to the articulations I use. Which notes are strong? Which are slurred? Which are short? Which are long?

Example 4c

You could analyse the previous three lines to see which scales and arpeggios they're built around, but I think it's better if you just start to use them. One way you could do this is to focus on the final hit point of each phrase and use that as the target note in your improvised melody variation. You don't have to use the whole phrase, just the part of it that stands out to you. Then play it around the changes of our workhorse tune.

Spend 20 minutes using the phrase to target the root of each chord. Then spend time targeting the 3rd and so on. You might have to alter the notes slightly, but your ears will tell you when that needs to happen. What's important is playing these pieces of vocabulary with confidence and the same articulation you hear on the audio track.

You know where your hit point is, and you know the vocabulary works… so it's simply a case of getting in the "woodshed" and making these ideas work. One good tip is to see where the starting note of the phrase lies in relation to the target note. For example, is it a scale tone above the 5th or a semitone below the 3rd? Then fill in the gaps with the line. Not every phrase will work on every chord tone, but you'll quickly figure that out.

Use the backing track and explore what sounds these phrases create.

Let's move on and begin to look at some of my language. We've touched on this before, but chromatics are an important part of most jazz lines. Here's one way I can move between the chords in our tune. Each one of the movements between the chord tones is a little piece of vocabulary in its own right. Take the one you most like the sound of and move it around the changes. Why not take the phrase on the final few notes and use that to target one hit point on each chord?

Example 4d

Here are some other pieces of the chromatic puzzle. Again, they snake their way around the chord changes, but each transition is a little piece of vocabulary in its own right. You could spend days exploring just these ideas.

Example 4e

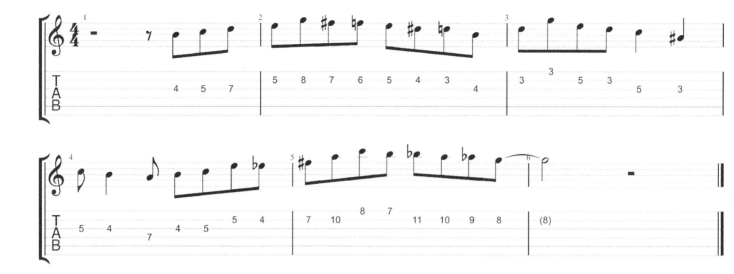

Now let's take add a little more complexity and take these ideas a bit further out.

Example 4f

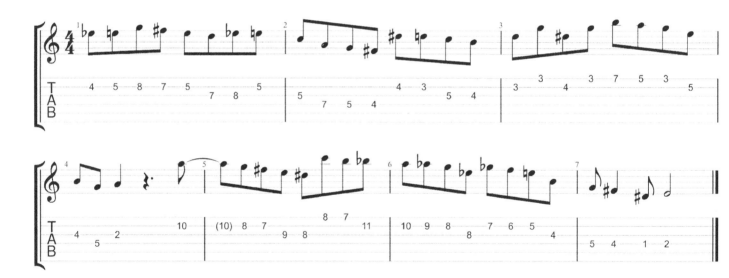

Here's a slightly longer improvisation packed with melodic ideas you can steal.

Example 4g

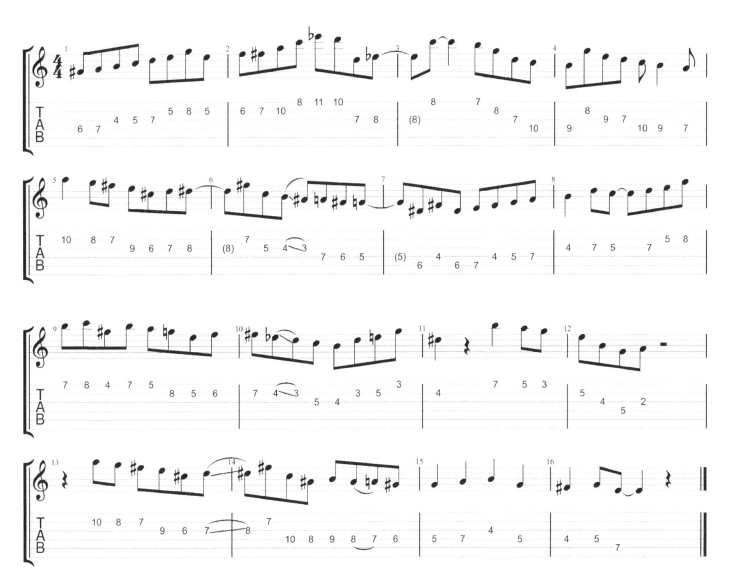

Finally here's another pass through the changes with some strong ideas based around trills. Notice how my improvisations led me to a little motif (the trill) that I locked onto and started to move around the chord changes. This is a very strong musical idea and you'll quickly start to develop themes in your solos if you do this. What's more, your audience will love you for it. Whenever you play an idea you like, repeat it and move it around the changes. This will help you to refine your melodic way of thinking and also sound great!

Example 4h

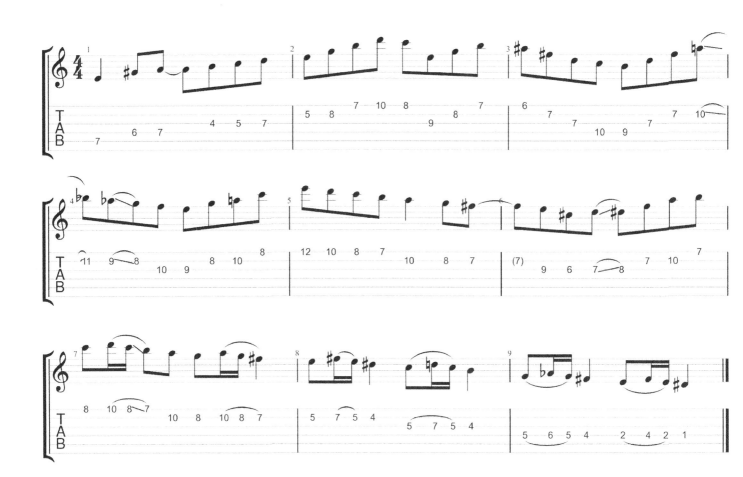

Think, Sing, Then Play

One of the dangers with the guitar is that our fingers take over when we play. This means we can quickly fall into playing pet licks that are part of our muscle memory and "programmed" into our body. It's common to hear my students' solos being led by the guitar, rather than them playing what they hear in their head, but this is like the tail wagging the dog!

The wonderful thing about jazz is that it works on any instrument because it is all about expressing the musical ideas we hear in our heads, and often a big part of my work when I'm teaching is to help the student take back control of the music. This is often a slow process because guitarists are so used to playing blues and rock licks they've memorised, rather than actually hearing the music first in their head and *then* playing it on the guitar.

For some reason, some people feel uncomfortable with the following set of exercises because they involve singing! I don't sing particularly well, but it doesn't matter – this isn't a singing exercise. Don't worry if you feel you can't sing, that's not the point.

This technique can make the biggest difference to your ability as a jazz soloist. It's about thinking of a melodic line, singing it, then playing it on guitar. This is a great discipline to develop. Not only will it help you to play the ideas in your head, it will dramatically improve your phrasing. Your lines will quickly take on a vocal quality that is missed by the majority of guitarists.

The following exercises will help you get started. (Feel free to change the key of the following exercises if they don't work for you at this pitch).

We'll begin with something simple and first of all, we'll flip the process around. Begin by playing the G Major scale and triad on your guitar. Then, without your guitar, sing up and down the scale and triad you've just heard.

Example 4i

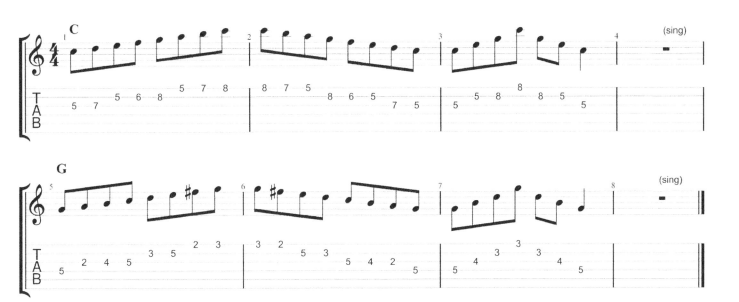

Now you're established your "territory", sing a very simple phrase of just a few notes and play it back on your guitar. Don't worry if you don't repeat it perfectly at first – it just means your ears aren't quite connected to your guitar yet. Figure it out note by note if you need to and the connection will come. Each note I sing in the following examples is taken from the eight note G Major scale, so you know the answers are in there somewhere.

Example 4j1

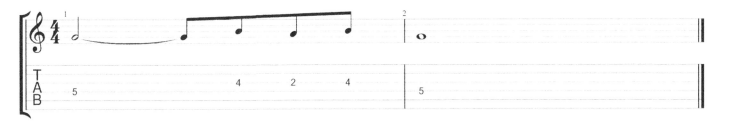

Example 4j2

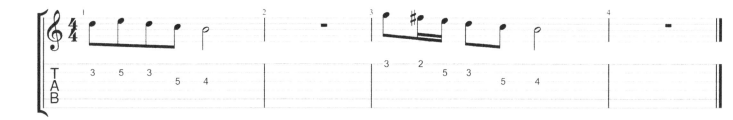

Example 4j3

Now it's your turn. You can spend hours doing this and it works as a great warmup every morning before you pick up your guitar. In your head, conceive some simple phrases using just the notes of the major scale, *then sing them*, then play them back on the guitar. You'll gradually begin to feel the connection between the music you hear in your head and what you play on the guitar grow stronger.

Soon, you'll want to get a little bit more adventurous and add slightly bigger jumps into your melodies.

Example 4k1

Example 4k2

This melody adds a chromatic note.

Example 4k3

Keep practising this exercise every day and very slowly begin to introduce bigger jumps and one or two chromatic notes. It's a lifetime pursuit and you'll learn to love it!

Remember the process: think what you want to play, *then* sing it, *then* play it.

Don't worry that when you begin there is a gap between what you sing and what you can reproduce on the guitar – you're working on establishing the connection between the melody you sing and where those notes are located. As long as you keep doing it, this gap will continually get smaller. Before long, you'll be able to play exactly what you hear in your head in real time.

When you combine this skill with all the vocabulary you've been learning, the vocabulary will begin to influence the lines you "hear" and your jazz soloing skills will quickly compound. In fact, at this point you can really stop worrying about scales and theory, because the lines you hear, sing and play will always work!

I've included a video of the next example to show you exactly how I think about singing and playing. Here's a transcription of what I play on the video but you should go and check it out here: **https://geni.us/singlenote**

Example 41

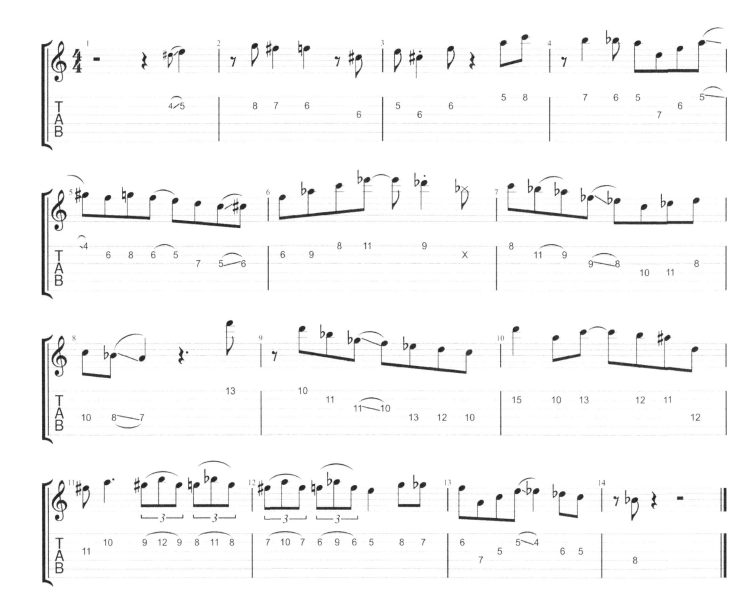

There are other ways to practise this skill. One great way is to find a vocal melody you like (it doesn't have to be jazz) and sing a phrase along with the record. Then turn the track off and sing the phrase again. Figure out the key of the song and play the phrase on your guitar. Again, you'll make mistakes, but don't worry, you'll make mistakes for the rest of your life – I know I do! The point is to hear the melody, sing it, then play it. If there are associated chord changes, you can figure them out too, but your primary goal is to sing, then play the melody.

A great bass player I worked with, Peter Ind, often didn't let his students get their instruments out of their cases and whole lessons were devoted to hearing then singing melodies to improve the student's vocabulary.

Another important approach is to transcribe parts of melodies and solos that you like, then sing them. This is a really good way to develop your own jazz vocabulary and again, links strongly to the way you learned to speak. I can't stress enough that *singing is the bridge* between the melodies you hear and actually being able to play them on the guitar in real time. It's called ear training because our ears *can be trained!*

Ultimately, the goal is to bypass the singing part and immediately play what you hear in your head. Singing is purely a device to close the gap. An old Buddhist saying visualises the process as crossing a river. We are on one bank (thinking) and we want to get to the other bank (playing). We can use a boat (singing) to get there, but once we're on the other shore, we've reached our destination – we don't need the boat anymore.

Phrasing and Articulation

Compared to many instruments, playing the guitar is a very mechanical process. What I mean by this is, unlike the saxophone, trumpet or voice, we can play the guitar constantly without any breaks because we don't need to take a breath to sound a note. While other instruments are *forced* to leave gaps in their lines due to their need to breathe, guitarists can go on all day! That's not really a good thing because there is a tendency to over-play.

This is another strong argument for learning to play jazz by listening to brass and woodwind players and bringing some of their phrasing approaches into our playing.

Think also about how a singer breathes. They sing a phrase, take a breath, then sing the next phrase. This naturally forms a two-line phrase which is often seen as a question and answer structure. It's something the listener naturally responds to and has the added advantage of helping you keep track of your place in the music. A two-bar question followed by a two-bar answer makes a four-bar line of music. If you do that eight times, it fills a 32-bar chorus. It might sound obvious, but guitarists often lose sight of that kind of structure in music, and this approach can really help you and your audience keep track.

When I learnt guitar I didn't really learn whole solos, I learnt phrases that I liked and that's something that has always underpinned my approach to playing. Thinking about *phrasing* not theory is vital, because when you think in terms of "these are the scales I can play on this chord" you really miss out on the musical, melodic aspect of playing jazz. Theory's useful, but not while you're improvising!

When you begin to think in terms of phrases to create melodies, you'll often find that one phrase you play suggests the next. Here's an example of a four-bar line split into two-bar phrases. Notice how the question phrase suggests an answer. Think about where a saxophone player would take a breath while playing this.

Example 4m

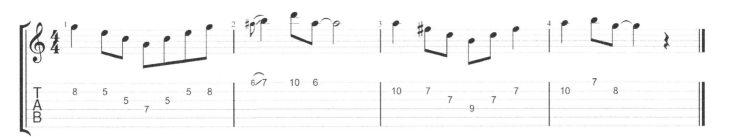

When I solo, I do actually breathe just like a horn player would. In fact, I only play when I'm breathing out. This stops me playing long "guitary" phrases without any break. Here's a short transcription of me playing that shows you where my breaths occur. (In the notation you'll see a * symbol which has been given a 1 beat rest. This is the pause for breath! I purposely overemphasise this pause on the audio example).

Example 4n

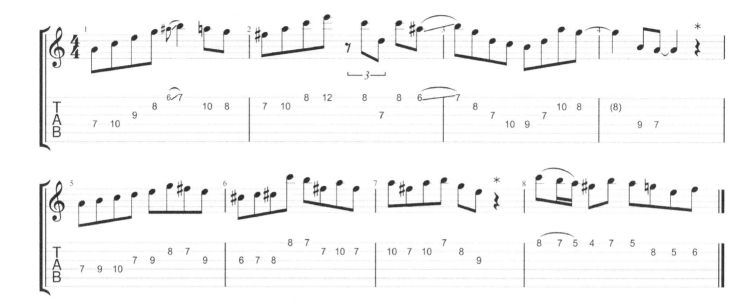

Breathing, thinking in phrases and learning vocabulary are all important factors in creating *poetic* phrases. When you focus on learning these skills you'll find that your jazz guitar playing quickly reaches a whole new level. When you speak, you breath. You use your vocabulary and talk in phrases to tell a clear story. The same is true in jazz soloing.

When you focus on phrasing, an unexpected benefit is that you automatically begin to incorporate *silence* into your playing. Sound and silence are two sides of the same coin. Think about when a seasoned actor delivers a monologue – their pauses create as much impact as their words. Silence in a story is essential because it allows the listener to process the information they've just heard. Don't forget to use plenty of silence in your solos to make your phrases stand out. You'll be a better player for it.

One final ingredient we must add to the recipe of good phrasing is *articulation*. Some guitarists like to give each note of their solo the same articulation by picking every note evenly. While that can work for some players, I prefer to mix up my articulation by picking some notes and using legato (hammer-ons and pull-offs) to give my phrases a smoother flow. The notes I do pick can really jump out compared to the legato notes, and this introduces a whole new textural dimension to my lines.

Here's a line that I first play by picking every note, then play with my normal style of mixing up the articulation. Each pick is marked and all the slurs are shown by the curved lines.

Example 4o1

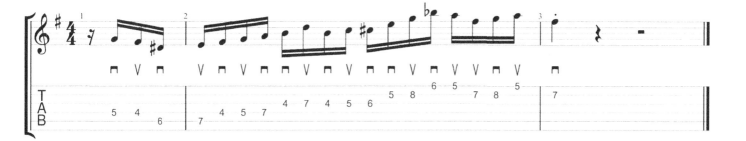

Example 4o2

The key here is experimentation and finding your own approach to articulating your phrases. Listen to great horn players and the musicians you love. Listen to the dynamics of their lines and see how their articulation brings out the nuances of the music.

Chapter Five – Swing, Rhythm and Timing

When I first started working as a guitarist, I was lucky enough to get to play with some really great players. However, working musicians tended to be tough guys and they were quite hard on us youngsters. Playing the odd wrong note or forgetting your place in the tune were forgivable offences – but the biggest crime you could commit was not playing in time. It didn't matter how well you could play or what clever ideas you came up with, if you didn't play in time you didn't last long in the band.

While playing behind the beat was a little better – especially in jazz – playing too far behind was equally frowned upon.

Reflecting on this now, I can see these guys had a point. In real life, your audience will respond much more to groove and a strong rhythm than the actual pitches you play. It gives them an anchor for the music. No one leaves a gig humming a rhythm, but equally no one dances to just a melody. When the band is cooking, you can see the audience begin to move, sway, clap their hands and maybe even dance!

Time and feel is purely physical. This means that you shouldn't just count along to your metronome, you should *move* along to it too. Tap your foot, nod your head, sway, or do them all – but whatever you do, make sure you have a physical connection to the beat. After all, that's why musicians call it having great feel! When you've been playing music for a long time you can feel the rhythm in your body; it becomes like a heartbeat.

My advice is before you play a note, spend time setting the time and locking into the feel. Listen to the band or your metronome and physically feel the rhythm before you play. Also do something physical, like tapping your foot, so that the pulse isn't just something in the airwaves, it becomes part of your body.

Listening skills

Once you've developed the habit of locking into a rhythm before you play, the next most important skill to develop is listening – both to other musicians and yourself.

Listening to what your fellow musicians are playing in a band setting is important in any genre of music, but especially so in jazz, which relies heavily on improvisation and interplay. If you can open your ears and pick up on what other instruments are playing, you can mirror their rhythms and lock in with their ideas. Audiences love to hear the interplay between musicians, when the guitar begins to play the same rhythms as the drummer or pianist. They'll think you've rehearsed these ideas, even though you're just interacting on the fly!

I've also found, however, that we are often guilty of not listening to *ourselves* very much. Some musicians are guilty of not listening to every note they play and can quickly lose touch with the effect they are having on their audience. If we're not mindful of what we're playing, we can also lose our grip on that inner metronome and fail to lock into the groove.

The easiest way to combat this is to record your practice and performances and listen back to them later. You'll often find that you were rushing or maybe you didn't sound as good as you thought (although don't be surprised if you sound better!) Don't be down-hearted if you hear something you don't like in your playing, though. This is a positive step because it allows you to focus on and improve something you didn't even know existed.

Mastering swing

Playing with great time and feel in other musical genres (such as funk) is often called playing "in the pocket". Jazz has its own version of playing in the pocket called *swing*. You can consider it a great compliment if anyone tells you they enjoyed your playing because "you can really swing."

However, swing is notoriously impossible to notate in music, and it's even a little difficult to describe it in such a way that you'll immediately get it. Swing is more art than science. That said, I've created some exercises that will help you to move from playing "straight" to playing with "swing" in a great jazz feel. You will need to listen carefully to the audio of these examples to hear the swing feel develop. (If you've not downloaded it yet, you can get it from **www.fundamental-changes.com**).

Example 5a is a melody based on the tune you learnt earlier to the changes of *Autumn Leaves*. Here the melody is played with zero swing – it is completely straight.

Example 5a

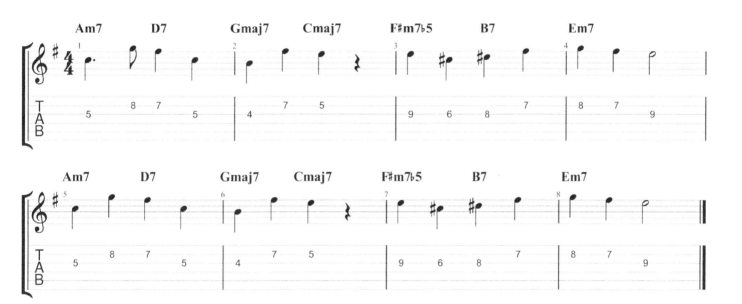

Here is the same melody, but now, quite subtly, I'm starting to swing. Notice that I'm not simply playing the same melody with a bouncy feel. It's the varied placement of the notes that creates the strong rhythmic feeling. Sometimes I'm anticipating the beat, playing notes slightly before it, and sometimes I'm playing behind the beat.

Example 5b

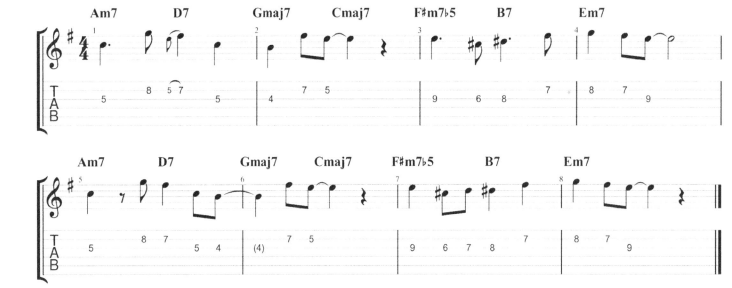

If I could describe it in one sentence, it's this pushing and pulling effect that is the essence of swing. In Example 5c notice that in the first four bars, I'm pulling the beat back by playing quite far behind it. It almost makes you feel awkward! But following this tension comes a release in the subsequent four bars, where the phrasing is still swinging, but the notes are played more on the beat.

Example 5c

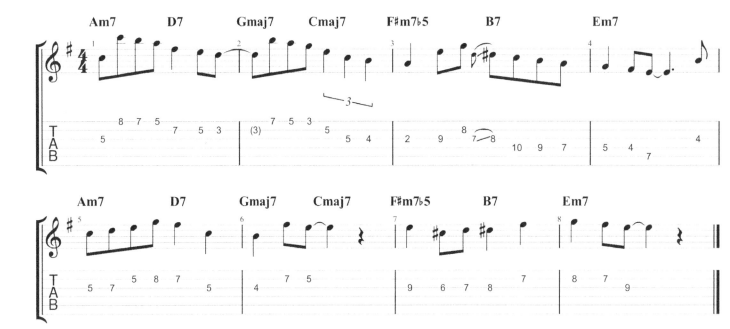

If you've been disciplined enough to record yourself playing to a metronome, you'll have noticed that the metronome is unerringly monotonous – it's supposed to be! It's perfectly in time. To create swing, you need to go a little off-kilter timewise and work around it. In Example 5d, I'm deliberately playing behind the beat in order to highlight what I mean.

Although the metronome is mathematically accurate, you can create the illusion that the time is swinging by pulling against it. Listen carefully to the audio example and you'll hear the interplay between the melodic line and the click.

Example 5d

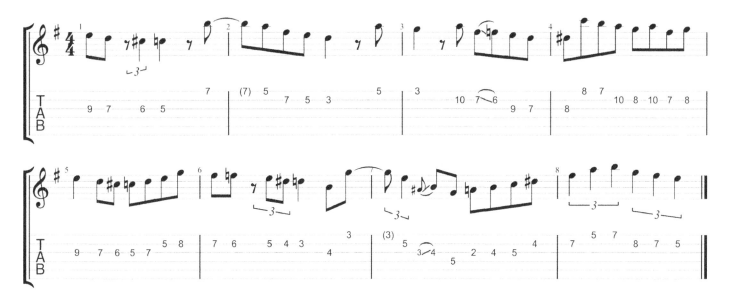

I'm now embellishing the simple melody I began with by adding other scale and chromatic notes, and in the longer example that follows I'm illustrating how you might freely pull and push as you play to create a sense of movement and direction. Now we're not just playing notes, we're beginning to tell a story – and it's swinging.

Example 5e

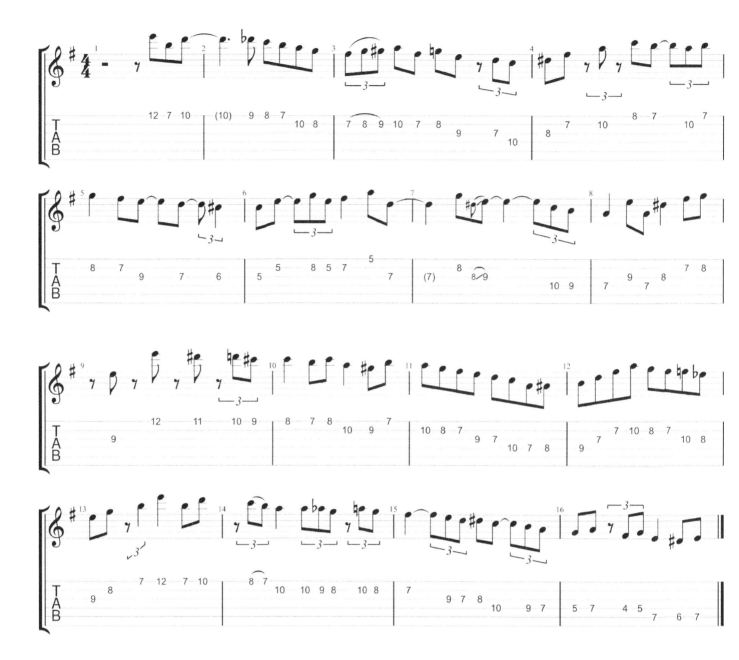

I'm sure you can hear the difference between something that's played totally straight and something that's swung, but how can one develop this skill?

When I play, I am consciously holding back certain phrases and playing them slightly late. When you first begin to practise this, it may feel like you're simply playing with bad time. Don't worry, this is normal! Record yourself and listen to where you are placing the notes. We guitarists have a tendency to rush and can often be straining against the beat. If you focus on playing notes just a fraction later than normal and listen back, you'll invariably find you're playing with a much better feel.

As well as consciously holding back, I also have target notes that I hit. This time I'm not targeting chord tones, I'm targeting *beats*. When I stretch time like an elastic band, pulling against the beat, I'll also hit certain notes dead on the beat.

When you are really comfortable and feel on top of the time, you can choose to target any beat you like, but in order to practice this skill, you should begin by targeting a specific beat over and over. In this short example I'm targeting the first beat of bar one and bar three.

Example 5f

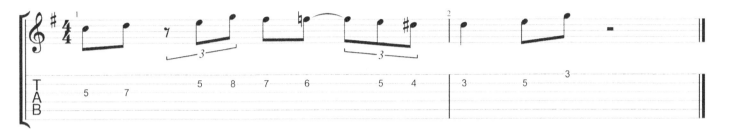

Set your metronome to around 60bpm and play any phrases you like, but ensure that you hit beat 1 of every other bar, dead on. For now, it doesn't matter what you do in between as long as you hit those beats perfectly. If you practise this diligently, eventually it will stop feeling like an exercise and begin to sound natural – and your time and feel will have improved dramatically!

Here is a longer example:

Example 5g

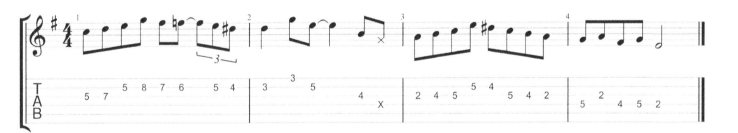

What I want you to take from this is that swing isn't just about playing the second 1/8th note later, it's about how you place the notes in the whole of the phrase. It's about relaxing and sitting behind the beat, making the pulse physical and listening to your rhythm section.

Here is one final example – a transcription of a spontaneous solo I played to demonstrate my swing feel and phrasing over a longer piece of playing. Work through it and pay particular attention to which beats I'm targeting and which notes are pushed or pulled.

Example 5h

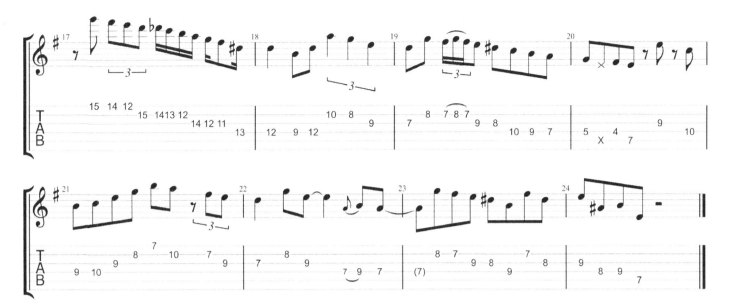

Chapter Six – Playing Out of the Box

When you first learned scales on the guitar, you probably did so with "box" shapes across the neck. These are useful to get going, but one thing I've found over the years is that it's much more useful to play up and down the neck, rather than with my hand locked into a single position on the guitar.

Playing up and down the neck makes it a lot easier to follow chord progressions because there's always a root note on the sixth or fifth string we can move to, and it stops us getting locked into the same ideas and reaching for the same scale shapes. I find that I'm much more creative as a jazz guitarist when I can freely ascend and descend the neck.

In Chapter One, I showed you how to play root and 10th voicings up and down the neck, and the ground we'll cover in this chapter ties in closely with that framework.

Let me illustrate the difference in approaches. For example, here's a line played in one position. I feel quite "trapped" while playing this and my line feels a bit predictable and limited by range.

Example 6a

In the next example, I begin the line in the same way, but allow myself to change position on the neck to tackle some of the chords. Immediately I feel freer and you'll notice that the melody not only feels more comfortable, it allows me to access a much greater range of the guitar.

Example 6b

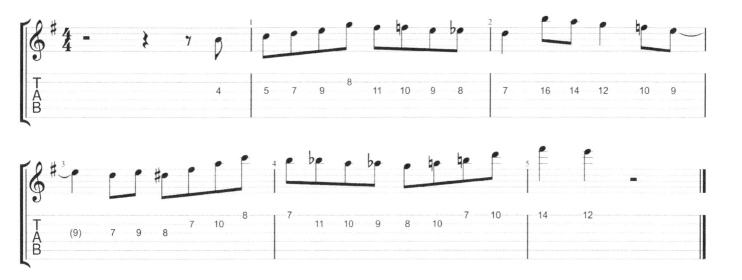

When I play the line above, I visualise the following chord shapes and build my lines around them. Of course, the shapes do jump around the neck, but the more you start to practice like this, the easier you will find it to join up these ideas and fill in the "no man's land" in between.

Example 6c

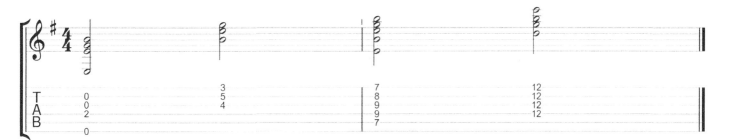

When guitarists play in one area of the neck all the time, one undesired result is that the music becomes quite one dimensional in its range. It's important to realise that the *register* we play in affects the *feeling* of the notes. Intervals played very low on the guitar are quite dark and dense, and intervals played high on the neck tend to be much lighter and brighter in colour. While the intervals are the same, playing them in a different range is like being able to paint in different shades of the same colour.

To demonstrate this idea, here is our tune played in three different registers. You'll instantly hear the difference.

Example 6d

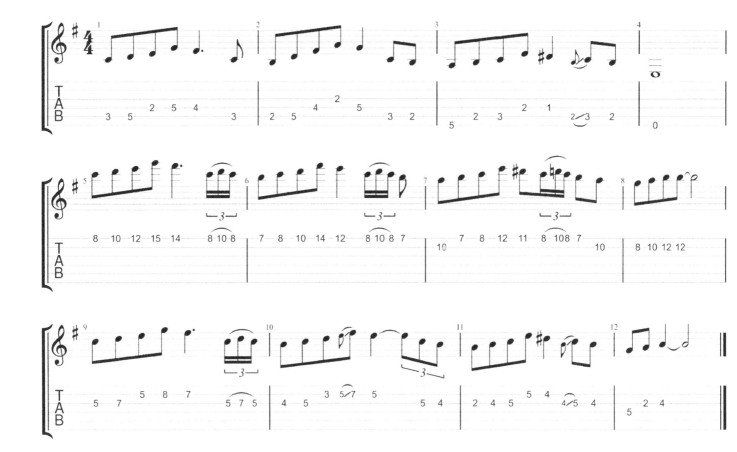

The dimension of colour is so important for both expression and for engaging that listener that I'm quick to notice its absence. Building freedom with range up and down the neck is a very important concept to practise.

I can use range deliberately to influence the mood of the solo. Here's a short example on that begins high, and then moves to a lower range to create a feeling of thoughtfulness and reflection.

Example 6e

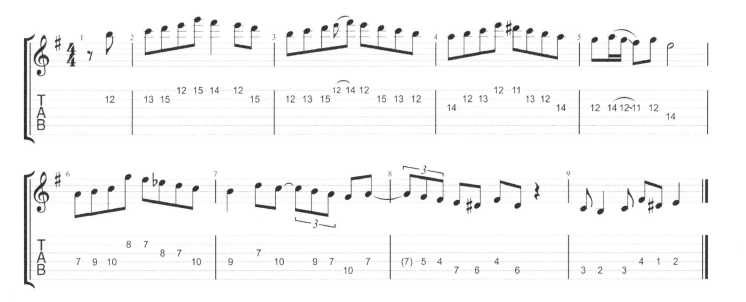

He's an example that achieves the opposite effect. I begin low and move to a higher register to add excitement and drama.

Example 6f

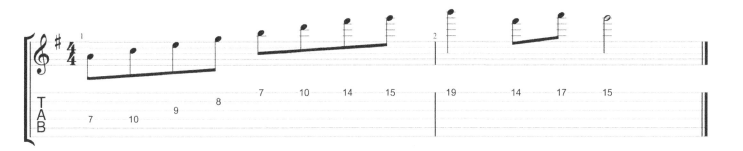

These colours are subtle, but they connect with your audience on a deep emotional level. They're an important tool in your musical kit box and are often forgotten in the pursuit of finding the perfect theoretical device to apply to a Bb7#9b13 chord!

Range is a valuable tool you can use to plan out your melodies and solos. As we've seen, it can be used to create a reflective mood or one of excitement. So, how can you practise using range? A wonderful exercise that will help you master it is to play a solo using *only one string*. This can be hard at first, but it will force you to do two very important things:

1. It will make you use the range of the guitar

2. It will make you think more carefully about your choice of note and phrasing

Here's an example of me improvising a solo played entirely on the B string.

Example 6g

Here are another few passes around the changes using this approach.

Example 6h

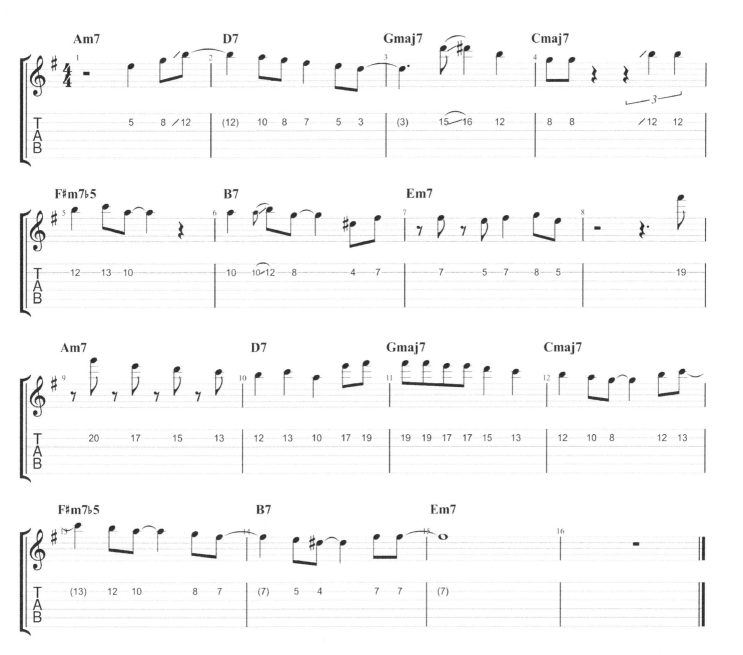

You can apply the idea of playing one just one string to your *think, sing, play* practice. It's a great way of discovering where the notes are located if you sing a phrase, then replicate it on just one string. It frees you from the distraction of familiar scale patterns and arpeggios which are easy to fall into.

Here's an example of me singing and playing a melody, again on the B string.

Example 6i

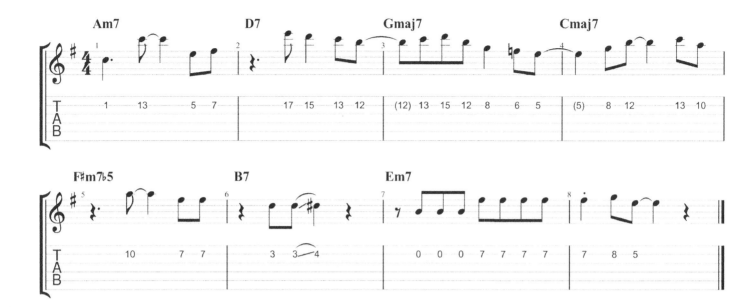

You should, of course, do this on different strings, although it might be good to limit yourself to the top four to begin with. Here's me playing a solo on the D string to help you find the locations of the notes.

Example 6j

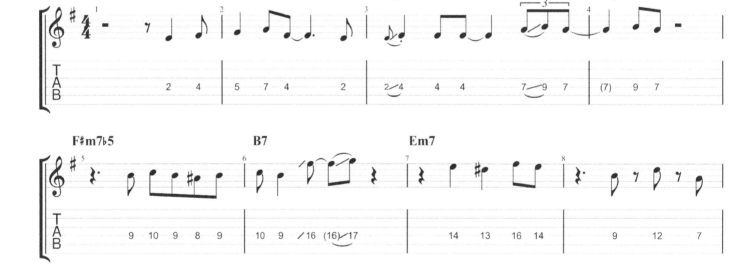

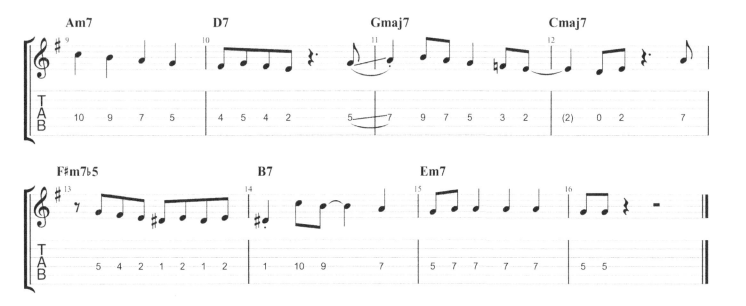

Try the *think, sing, play* method on the D string now. This is so important because you'll stop trying to find the scales and instead focus on finding the notes you hear in your head.

Example 6k

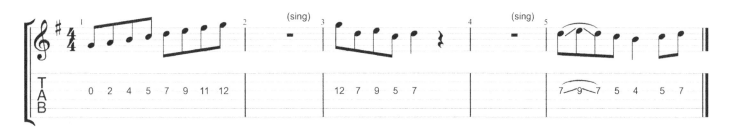

Ultimately, where I choose to play comes down to tone and feel. We know that there is more than one location to play a pitch on the guitar, and they all have a subtly different feel and texture. I learnt his from Stéphane Grappelli who did this a lot on the violin. He'd often repeat phrases on different strings to create subtle nuances in tone, like this:

Example 6l

I'd like to make one last point in conclusion. As well as using the range of the instrument, the *key* you choose to play a song in is an important consideration. When I'm playing solo guitar, I'll often transpose tunes to more guitar-friendly keys. Not just because it allows me access to open strings for bass notes, but because of the over sound those keys convey.

Sharps keys, such as E, A and D, have a bright, happy sound, while flat keys such as F, Bb and Eb sound darker. The guitar is engineered to be play the sharp keys optimally, so it's no wonder they sound a little sweeter. This is another way of saying you should always bear in mind what mood, what colour, you want to communicate to your listeners. Think about which key really brings a tune to life or gives it the mood you're after, and use the full range of the instrument, so that your improvisations sound three-dimensional and are always going somewhere.

Chapter Seven – Creating Interest and Structure in your Solos

We've talked in great detail about different ways to create a jazz guitar solo. These have mainly focused on keeping in mind specific target notes and using creative ways of navigating between them. But there is another important dimension in jazz soloing that is often overlooked and rarely taught: how to *pace* a solo. *Pacing* is one of the key ingredients that will keep your audience engaged and eager to hear what comes next. What do we mean by *pacing*?

Let me use the analogy of a TV programme. A well-written TV show develops. It has a structure that gradually increases in tension, introduces new ideas and has emotional highs and lows. It has loud parts and quiet parts and other features that make it more than the sum of its parts. Pacing how these ingredients can be used effectively is the mark of a good storyteller. A good scriptwriter will know how they want the narrative to unfold: what emotions will be stirred 5 minutes; 10 minutes in; how the show will come reach its pinnacle before the credits roll…

This is exactly how to structure a great jazz solo. It sounds obvious to say it, but if you come out with all guns blazing, then you have nowhere left to go. A sound grasp of pacing will allow you to take your audience on a journey that has lows and highs and develops in an organic manner.

How does one learn to do this?

My advice is that just as we've focused on *melodic* hit points in our solos, we can target *dynamic* hit points. By "dynamics" I mean more than just playing loudly and quietly. For me, dynamics includes light and shade, but also the amount of space you leave, the density of notes you play, the speed at which you play, the intervals you target, and the intensity of your playing.

Just like the screenwriter, you can have these devices ready at hand and plan when you'll use them. Targeting a *dynamic hit point* is, for instance, knowing ahead of time that over the course of three choruses you will hit a peak where you are in the upper range of the fretboard and your note density will be high, as you place a fast, repeating motif. Knowing that you want your solo to peak here, you can gradually build the intensity of your improvisation over the choruses leading up to that hit point.

Having the "big picture" of the solo you want to play in your mind, rather than getting caught up in the minutiae of which notes to play or which scales to use is very freeing. It's a flexible approach. Some players think of their solos in terms of which licks/scales they'll use when over the chords. This can work, but considering the endless variables at work during a live performance, often things don't go to plan, and if you miss a note or lose your place, the entire performance can fall apart.

Dynamic hit points offers a simpler, more liberating approach. You might say to yourself, for instance, "I'll begin with a few spaced-out light phrases that gradually grow, then take it down towards the bridge. After that, I'll begin to build it up and really start revving it up towards the end of the solo. Instead of a big finish, this time I'll reduce the intensity to give the next soloist a platform to grow from."

Now we've captured the overall architecture and mood of our solo without getting bogged down in specifics. If you rigidly plan your solo around licks, you'll have no room for manoeuvre in a fast-moving, creative musical environment; no safety net. With dynamic targeting, you can always quickly adapt your approach to respond to what's happening around you.

Wrong notes?

Making mistakes can often throw musicians off course. If you're only playing licks, you'll probably have to stop if you make a mistake because you'll be locked into the phrase that has gone wrong. If you're not locked into licks, then if you make a mistake (I don't even call them mistakes, I call them "notes I didn't mean to play"), you can always adapt – even embrace the note you didn't mean to play and take the solo in a whole new direction.

Think of it this way: any note you didn't mean to play is just a tension note. It's only one fret away from a better note. If you can think of it like this, you'll begin to realise that "wrong notes" are another opportunity to be creative. If you resolve a "wrong note" strongly, then it will take your solo on a new, original path.

Often, I'll try to encourage myself to play notes I didn't mean to by playing songs in different keys, so I can't rely on my old patterns. Knowing that my new opportunities are endless, it actually helps me to relax when I solo. I embrace these notes and use them creatively.

The biggest mistake is to have your solo all figured out. It puts way too much pressure on you. When I play, I'm always thinking, "I don't know how this is going to turn out." I've got enough experience to know it's not going to be a total disaster, but embracing those notes is the secret to relaxing and being creative.

With all this in mind, let's look in detail at one way I structure a jazz guitar solo. The following examples break down a full solo transcription into small sections and begin with me just easing my way into the solo gently.

Example 7a

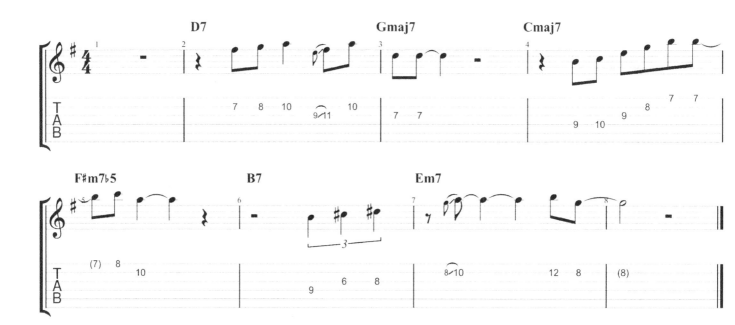

Here are the next few bars. Notice that I'm using a few melodic patterns already.

Example 7b

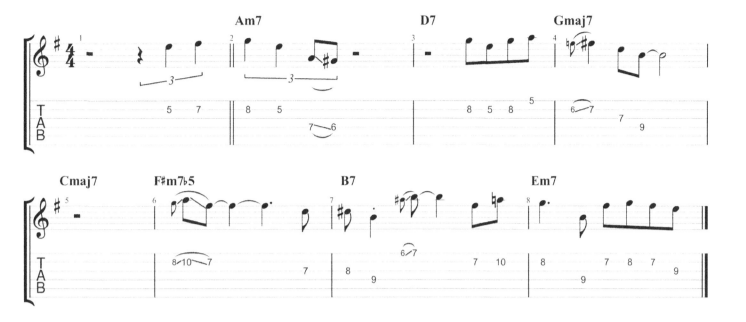

In the next example I lead with a strong motif that develops into a slightly busier phrase, using call and response.

Example 7c

I start building the intensity with volume, flurries of fast notes and dynamics.

Example 7d

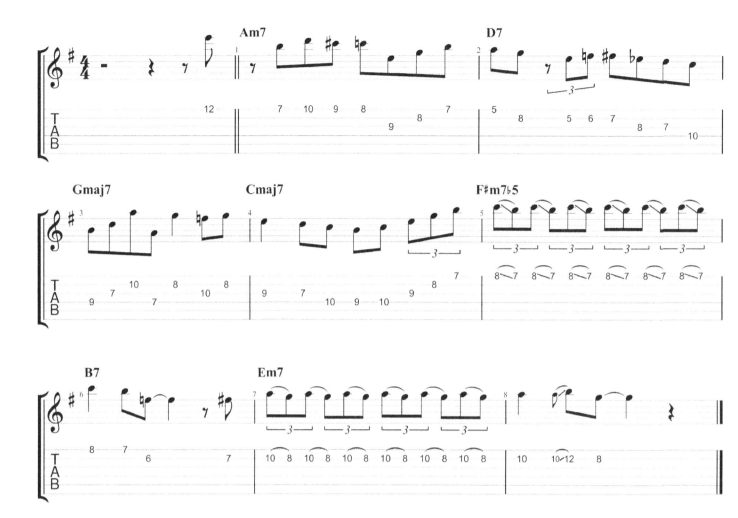

A strong motif sets me up to begin playing faster lines after a brief dip in intensity. The section ends with me reaching for some bluesy lines to balance out the faster phrases.

Example 7e

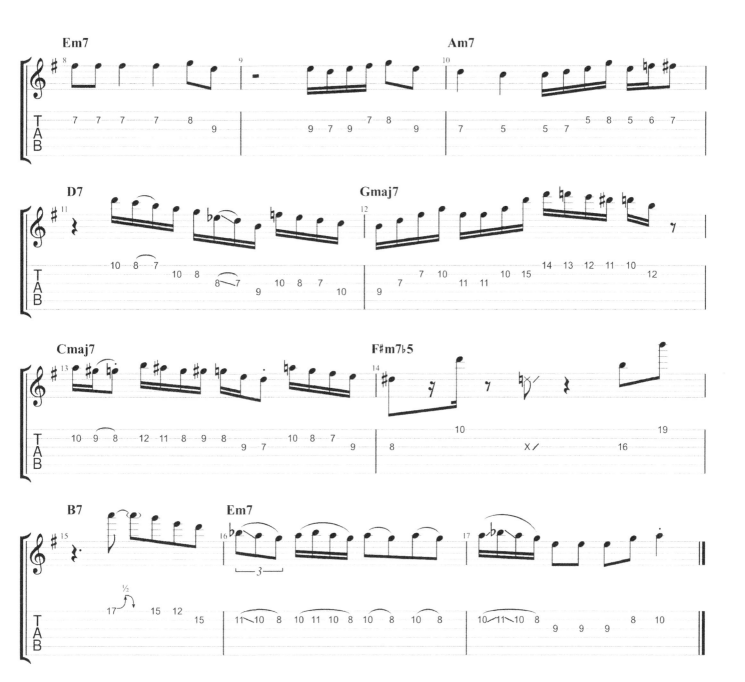

I begin the next section by combining different note durations, fast and slow, before I feel I need to balance the single note lines and introduce some octave textures.

Example 7f

Now I raise the intensity again with some fast scale and chromatic based lines, which I again balance with some bouncy swing, and reintroduce the octaves. The solo finishes with me lowering the energy, almost bowing out to leave the room, so a following soloist could begin their solo. Notice how I play softer *and* play fewer notes.

Example 7g

I'm sure you're wondering about some of those faster lines. These tend to be more scale based with chromatic notes filling in the gaps and targeting tones in the next chord. Really, I just double the amount I play on each chord. Here are a few ideas you can steal!

Example 7h

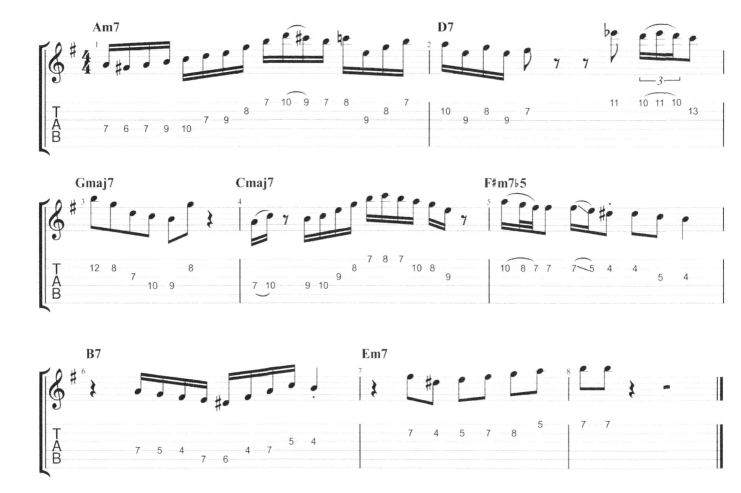

See how the fast phrases build tension while the slower phrases release it? This can work the other way around too, but fast then slow is a great starting point in your exploration of this idea.

Example 7i

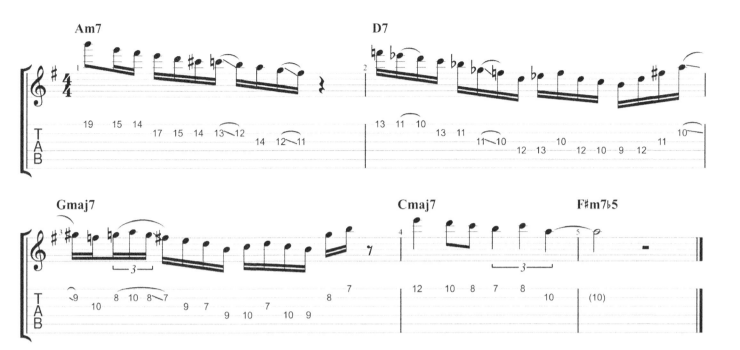

On the D7 chord, I often play the b9 (Eb) to create a slightly more tense sound. Here is some vocabulary that shows you how to do this.

Example 7j

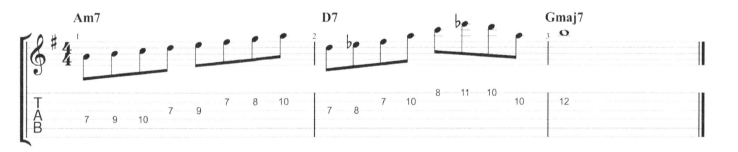

I hope this chapter has given you further insight and some tools to help you structure your solos and keep them interesting with pacing and dynamic hit points. Remember, it's not just what you play, it's a mindset. Plan ahead and have in mind the dynamics of your solo – the high points, the reflective points, the fast and slow, loud and soft. Embrace the notes you didn't mean to play and incorporate them into your variations because they'll take you in new creative directions you would never have imagined. Remember, when you play a note you didn't mean to, you're only ever one note away from a better one!

Chapter Eight – Piecing it all Together

We've covered a huge amount of ground in this book and many of the concepts will require months of work to perfect. I want to finish by applying all the concepts we've learnt into one complete solo. I'd like you to learn it, break down each idea and phrase to understand which notes I'm targeting, then compose your own variations on my lines. When I first learnt to play, I rarely memorised whole solos, I listened hard and figured out the lines I liked. I suggest you go through the solo and focus on learning the phrases that really leap out at you, then use them in your own playing as soon as possible.

In the following solo, you'll hear how I organically develop the initial melody using simple variations, then begin to stretch out a little as a soloist. Listen for my dynamics too and try to sketch out how the solo rises and falls in intensity. I begin with simple motifs.

Example 8a

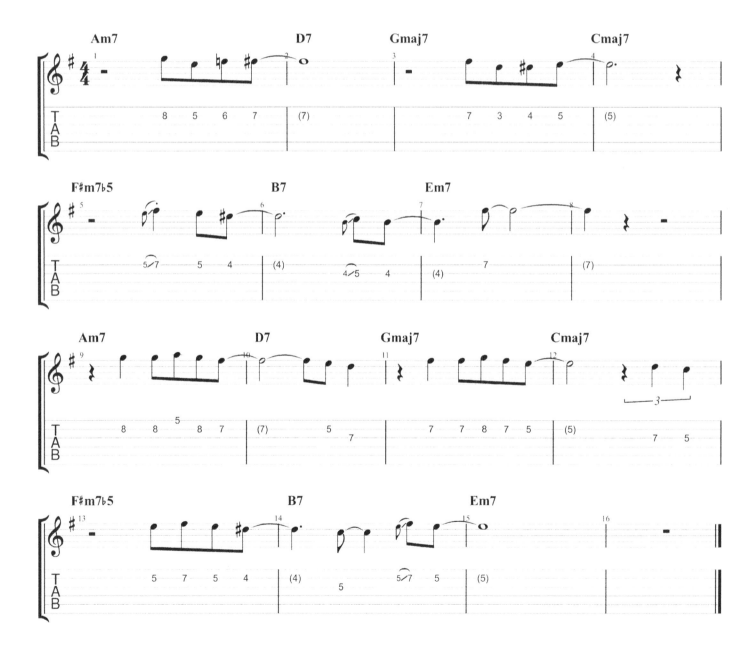

Then I begin to adapt a phrase I liked the sound of.

Example 8b

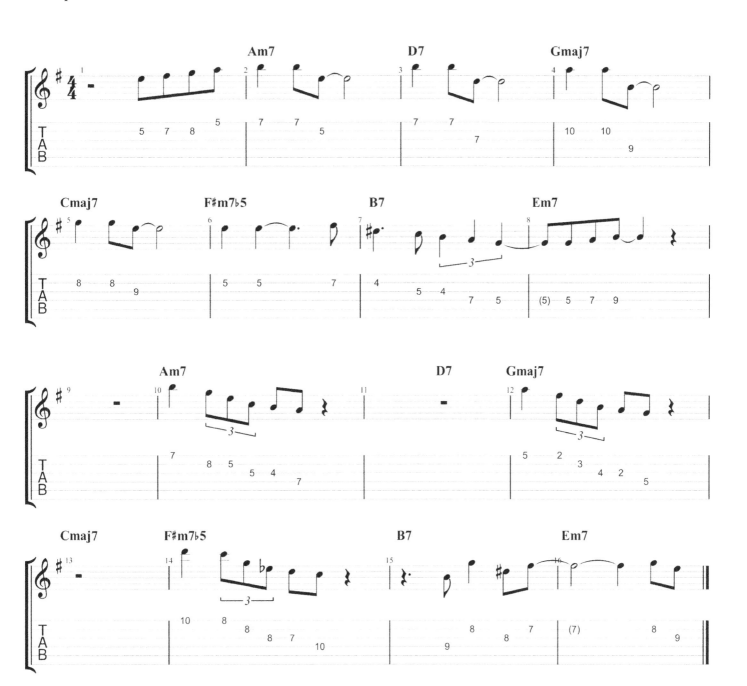

The next section uses a strong call and response idea.

Example 8c

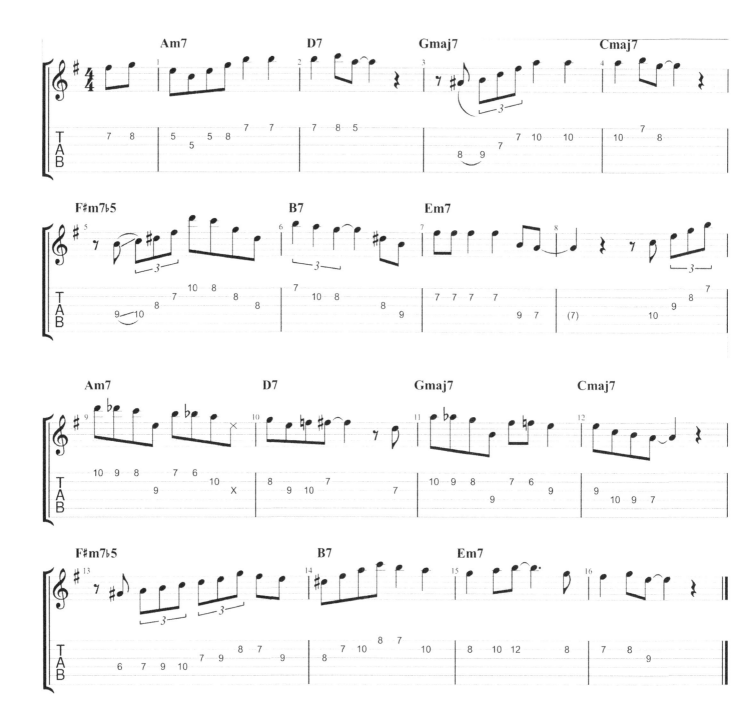

Hear how I develop some strong rhythmic patterns in the next few bars.

Example 8d

There are loads of repeating ideas in the next section that use different parts of the neck to demonstrate the use of range.

Example 8e

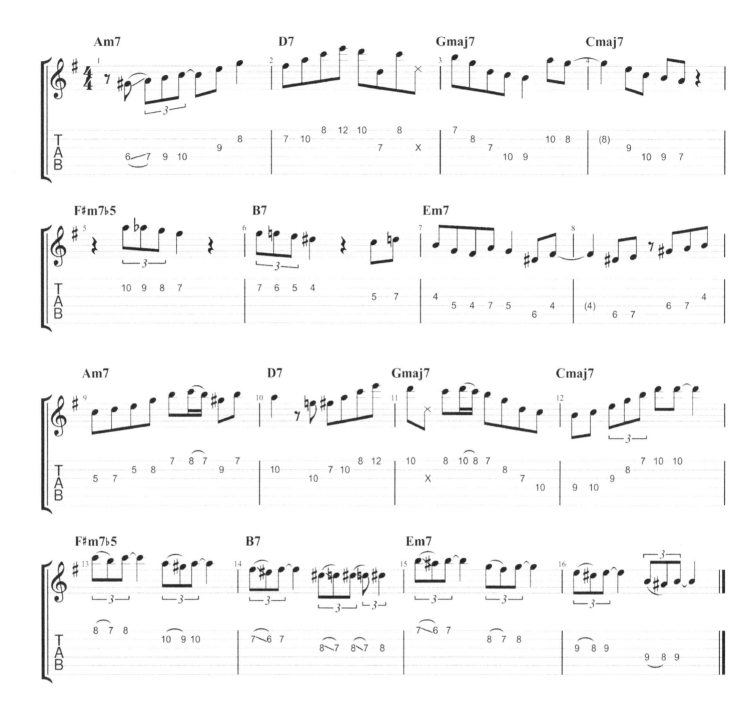

Now there is another mellow section before I play some flurries of chromatic notes to target chord tones.

Example 8f

OK, now it's over to you to break down and learn my next three choruses. Listen out for strong motifs being moved around the changes, using range, note intensity, dynamics, legato and of course variation of melodies.

Example 8g

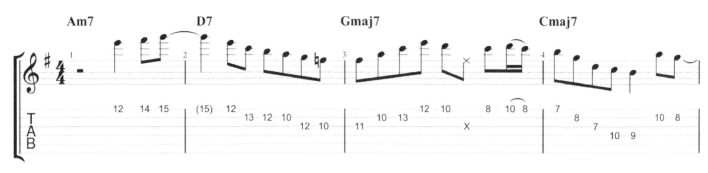

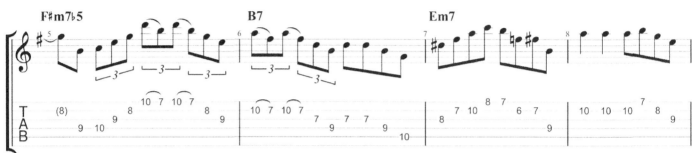

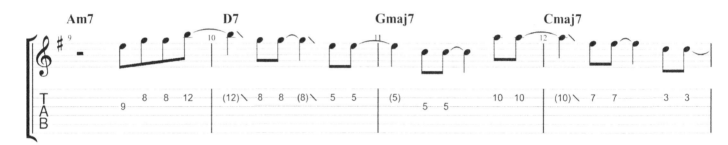

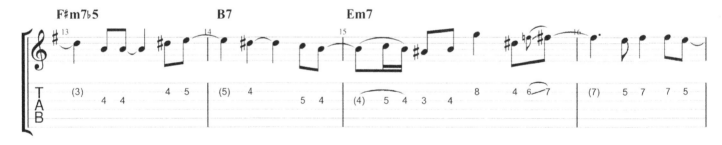

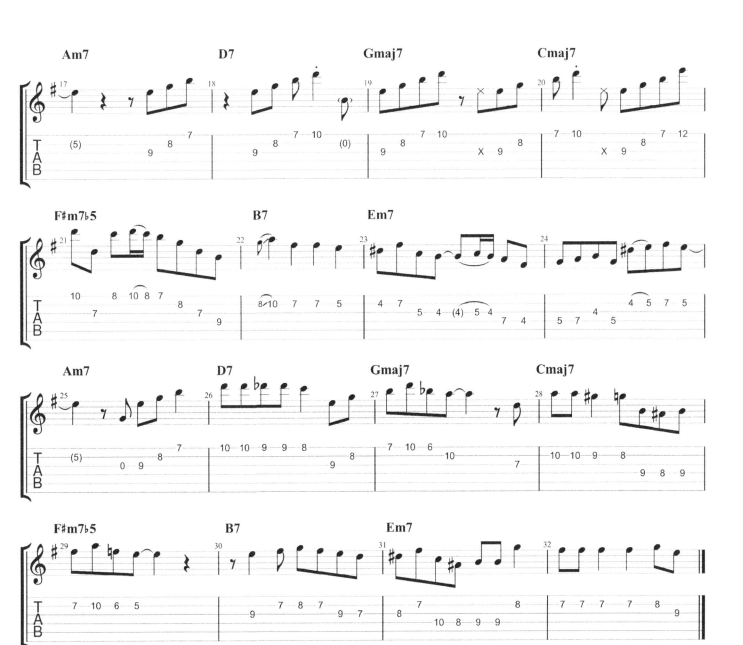

Example 8h

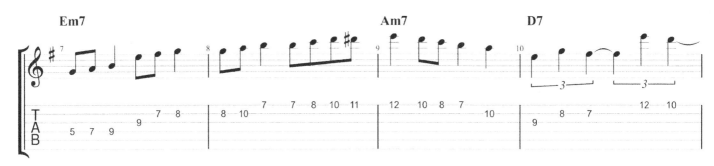

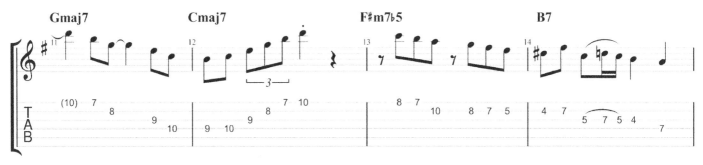

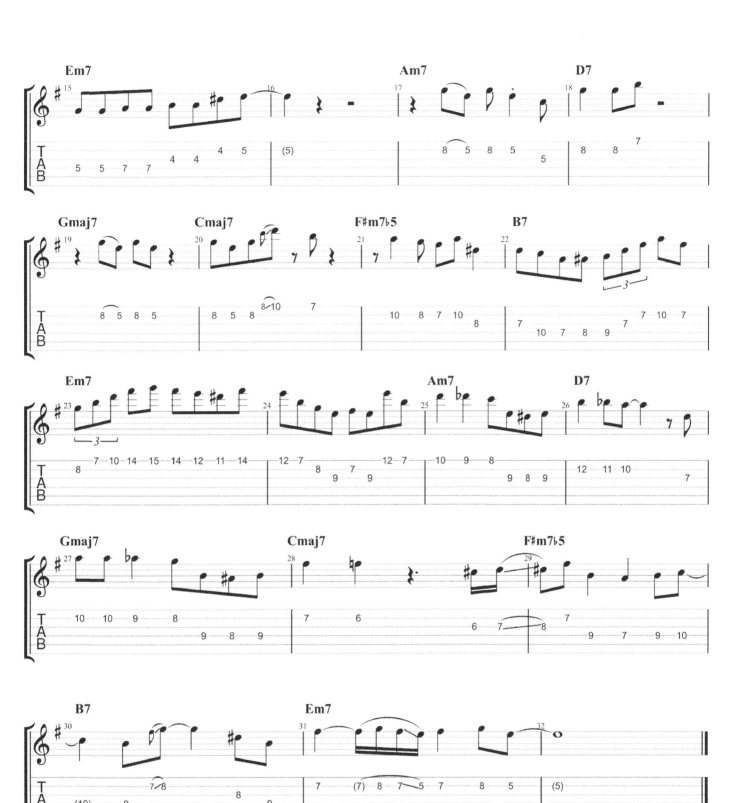

Example 8i

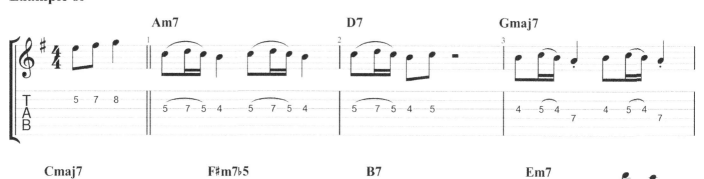

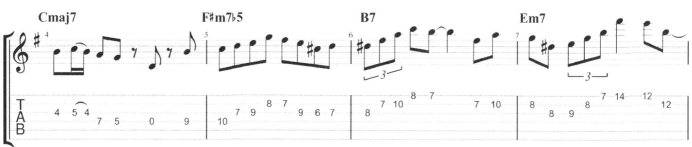

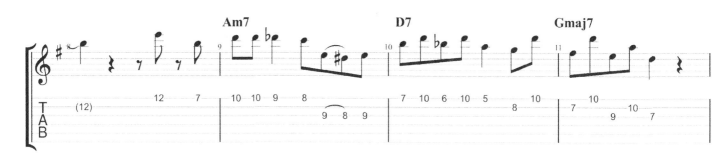

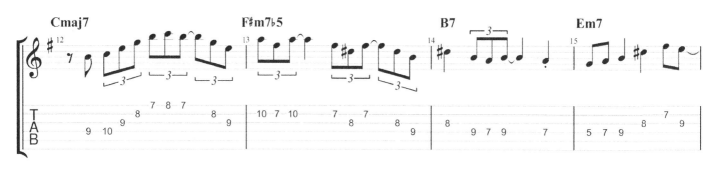

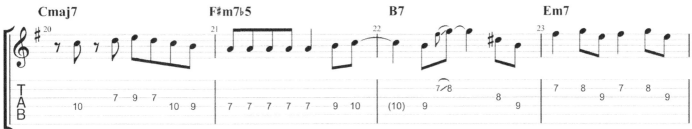

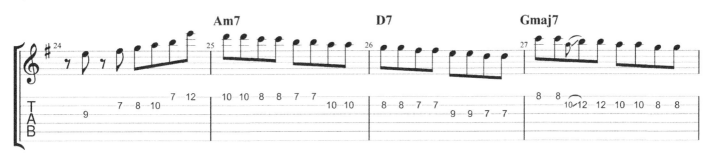

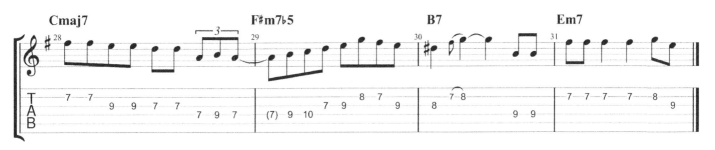

Conclusion and Further Reading

Congratulations, you made it!

I hope that what I've taught you in this book has given you a clear insight into the way I approach jazz guitar soloing. I've tried not to hold anything back and to explain my process as clearly as possible for you.

Remember, every solo begins by varying the melody of the tune and hearing those all-important hit points. When those are strong in your ears, you can target new intervals and take those variations further and further away from the original melody.

The golden rule to develop your jazz creativity and play whatever you hear in your head is to *think, sing then play*. If you practise this every day, your skills will quickly develop, and you will have much less reliance on "playing theory". Melody always comes first.

What I've taught you here will take you many years to perfect, but that's a good thing because the journey will be fun and you'll enjoy it. Don't be afraid to get out there and play as soon as possible. Find other musicians who are better than you and jam with them as much as possible – you'll get better much more quickly.

If you want more insight into my playing style, and want to learn how I play chords and basslines at the same time as soloing, I have two other books published through Fundamental Changes:

Beyond Chord Melody

and

Walking Basslines for Jazz Guitar

In them, I break down my approach to polyphonic playing and teach you the seven steps to chord melody mastery.

Also, look out for my new book of Christmas music arranged for chord melody guitar due to be released in November 2019. I think you'll get a lot out of it and it'll teach you my approach to arranging any song on guitar.

The most important rule in music is to always have fun and keep your mind open to new ideas and possibilities.

All the best,

Martin

Other Jazz Guitar Books From Fundamental Changes

100 Classic Jazz Licks For Guitar

Advanced Jazz Guitar Concepts

Fundamental Changes in Jazz Guitar

Jazz Bebop Blues Guitar

Jazz Blues Soloing For Guitar

Jazz Guitar Chord Mastery

Jazz Guitar Chord Tone Soloing

Martin Taylor – Beyond Chord Melody

Martin Taylor – Walking Bass for Jazz Guitar

Minor ii V Mastery For Guitar

Modern Jazz Guitar Concepts

Rhythm Changes For Jazz Guitar

The Jazz Guitar Soloing Compilation

The First 100 Jazz Chords For Guitar

The Jazz Guitar Chord Compilation

Voice Leading Jazz Guitar

Scan the QR code with your smartphone to discover more